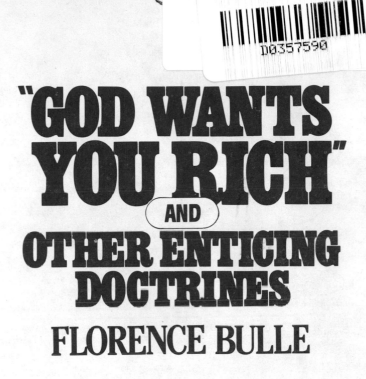

"GOD WANTS YOU RICH"
AND
OTHER ENTICING DOCTRINES

FLORENCE BULLE

BETHANY HOUSE PUBLISHERS
MINNEAPOLIS, MINNESOTA 55438
A Division of Bethany Fellowship, Inc.

Published by Bethany House Publishers
A Division of Bethany Fellowship, Inc.
6820 Auto Club Road, Minneapolis, Minnesota 55438

Printed in the United States of America

Bulle, Florence.
   God wants you rich, and other enticing doctrines.

   Bibliography: p.
   1. Christian life—1960-   I. Title.
BV4501.2.B835   1983   230   82-24460
ISBN 0-87123-264-2 (pbk.)

That their hearts might be comforted, being knit together in love, and unto all riches of the full assurance of understanding, to the acknowledgement of the mystery of God, and of the Father, and of Christ;

In whom are hid all the treasures of wisdom and knowledge. And this I say, lest any man should beguile you with enticing words.

Colossians 2:2-4 (KJV)

About the Author

FLORENCE BULLE, mother of four grown children, makes her home with her husband in Houghton, N.Y. She received a B.S. in Psychology from Houghton College and is working on her M.S. degree in Mental Health Counseling at Saint Bonaventure University. Mrs. Bulle writes from many years' experience in conference and retreat ministry. This is her second book.

To Dad,
Marshall Arthur Schoolcraft,
with love

Acknowledgments

When Pastor Harold Irish found himself in the pages of *Lord of the Valleys*, he wrote me, "Praise God for His wonderful love, and for the way He puts our lives together, that there may be ministry for His glory in lifting His children into His presence and its accompanying holiness!"

This book, too, reflects the way that God "puts our lives together" to accomplish His purposes. In one way or another, so many have helped that with heartfelt thanks I acknowledge them.

To Dr. Floyd McCallum—teacher, counselor, friend—whose vast experience and intimate walk with God have been a great encouragement to me. He has counseled, prayed, and cheered me on in my writing and, more important, in my own spiritual pilgrimage.

To Louise Prinsell whose delightful wit and wisdom I ever cherish. Her suggestions and positive criticism of the manuscript helped to bring it into focus. Her prayers and encouragement helped keep me at my typewriter.

To those whose struggles and pain I have shared; and yet, who must remain anonymous to protect their privacy.

To the many ministers—Carlton Spencer, Judson Cornwall, Stephen Olford, John Kimlingen, Mark Abbott, and others—who have remained true to the Word of God amidst the stormy controversies sweeping and ravaging the Body of Christ. I owe much to their encouragement, to their personal commitment to spiritual stability and biblical balance, and to their input into my life. I hope they will be pleased by what I have written.

To Liz Gibson and Charles Bressler who graciously shared their expertise.

Especially to my husband Al and daughter Jan, who worked hard at putting up with the writer-in-residence. Their prayers and support are priceless.

Finally, to all who have graciously spoken or written telling me how God used *Lord of the Valleys* to bring them under the lordship of Christ. And, to those who have expressed concern over the enticing doctrines threatening the reality of Christ's lordship over His children.

Together you have challenged me to endure the long, painful struggle of bringing this book to birth—I thank you.

—And this is my prayer: that your love may abound more and more in knowledge and depth of insight, so that you may be able to discern what is best and may be pure and blameless until the day of Christ, filled with the fruit of righteousness that comes through Jesus Christ—to the glory and praise of God. (Phil. 1:9-11)

Preface

Had anyone told me when I completed my first book, *Lord of the Valleys,* that it would be ten years before my next book and that it would deal with deception and bondage, I would have shaken my head and said, "No way!" I was all set to bear witness to the discovery of new dimensions of the lordship of Christ and to do it quickly.

But *Lord of the Valleys* opened unexpected doors of ministry—conferences, seminars, retreats, and personal counseling. Prodded by God, I went back to college, received my B.S. degree in psychology, and took a couple of graduate courses as well.

When I first turned up on the college campus, our sons—Marshall, Stephen, and Daryl—had already left the nest and were feathering their own. But our daughter, Janyce, was still at home. The fall after I graduated, she started the ninth grade at a Christian academy; thus my traveling still had to be limited. Yet I was getting around enough to wonderfully broaden my concept of the family of God. The powerful charismatic renewal had broken down long-standing walls; it was wonderful to get out and meet my Christian relatives I hadn't even known existed. Too, there was the unparalleled joy of seeing broken lives and bodies healed and transformed by the power of God. That my heavenly Father had let me be even a tiny part of the action set my soul to singing.

But before long, I gradually became aware something sinister was happening within the renewal movement. The early emphasis on Jesus as Lord and on His endowment of His Church with the power and gifts of the Holy Spirit was shifting, was being obscured. One new teaching after another—each with some unique emphasis—vied for top billing. Many of these teachings were based on valid biblical principles, but the principles were being twisted and pushed to excess. People were falling for distorted doctrines, and deception was taking a tremendous toll on some who had started out so well.

The alarm I felt plunged me into the most difficult writing project I have ever undertaken. And though I never would have believed it, while I struggled to turn out the chapters—frustrated by no end of wild interruptions—seven years whooshed by.

This time span, however, served to clarify some of the issues and confirm some of my early suspicions. It became evident that many of the popular theologies were promoted by magnetic personalities intent, whether consciously or unconsciously, on building their own kingdom—not God's. And they succeeded, in part, because many newly born of the Spirit were opening their Bibles for the first time. Not having a substantial knowledge of the Word, they didn't catch on when false teachings were fabricated from carefully selected scriptures that were often merely half-truths when they stood apart from the whole counsel of God from Genesis to Revelation. Even Christians more knowledgeable in the Word sometimes fail to recognize error camouflaged by a preponderance of truth. So, multitudes of sincere Christians have vigorously applauded men and movements promoting distorted doctrines seeded with deception.

Another thing. Christians tend to think of deception only in terms of Jim Jones or the Moonies or Scientology, or one of the more "respectable" cults such as Jehovah's Witnesses or Mormonism, or as any activity involving supernatural powers apart from Jesus Christ. Most know better than to play around with Ouija boards, *I Ching,* tarot cards, astrology, fortune-telling, witchcraft, and séances. But the catch is that the greatest threat to the born-again child of God does not come from the cults or the occult; it comes from Satan's more subtle strategy: distorted teaching *within the true Church.* It is my purpose to expose these enticing doctrines to the light of God's Word.

But before we begin, I must add one personal word.

Many times I have asked myself—and I am sure the thought has already occurred to many of you—"Who am I to tackle the giants?"

Oh, David! How I feel for you standing there with only a slingshot and five smooth stones! And your brothers scoffing at your audacity to take on Goliath.

But I also know what motivated you in that moment—a burning passion that the living God be not mocked. And that Jehovah's people not be taken captive by the enemy. You wanted them free.

That, too, is my motive. And I pray:

O Lord. Don't let us who are Your children wander off on by-paths of deception because we fail to discern the danger. Let us see with crystal clear vision the revealed truth of God.

For those who guide this people are leading them astray; And those who are guided by them are brought to confusion. (Isa. 9:16, NASB)

But when he, the Spirit of truth comes, he will guide you into all truth. (John 16:13, NIV)

If you hold to my teaching, you are really my disciples. Then you will know the truth, and the truth will set you free. (John 8:32, NIV)

Contents

Introduction

Itching Ears and Deceived Minds

The Enemy, throughout history, has basically resorted to three bags of clever tricks. One, to make the Church believe there is no devil; two, to cause the Church to be obsessed with the devil and his demons; three, to cause the Church to think she cannot be deceived.

Consider the first bag of tricks. During the eighteenth century, the Church was a pushover for Satan's deception that there is no devil. It was then that *rationalism* emerged as the new world view.

Revolutionary changes in science during the seventeenth century had set the scene by fostering a climate of distrust. Till then, the earth was believed to be the center of the universe, not merely a planet revolving around the sun. If man had so misunderstood the universe, "enlightened man" reasoned, was not his understanding of the Bible also suspect?

By the eighteenth century, rationalism had become the accepted principle. Revelation and the supernatural were rejected; belief in the devil was passé.

Denying the devil's existence, however, did not remove him from the scene. On the contrary, the old boy had a heyday. As the teachings of the Bible were watered down to keep in step with contemporary thought, so the "holy passion" of the Church was dissipated. Philosophers and theologians became the devil's

15

stooges. If and when the supernatural occurred, they shrewdly explained these phenomena away in a manner agreeable to human reason. The devil's existence was not deleted from Church dogma, but for the most part belief in his being was written off— at least by the historic churches.

Today there is a growing recognition by the scientific community of spiritual forces beyond those perceived by the five senses. And once again the Church is taking the devil seriously.

Ironically, though, it is not the Church recovered from her heresies and functioning in a supernatural dimension which has caught the attention of the scientists. Nor has the exposure of Satan and the demonic world come from the children of light. Rather, the chief catalyst awakening scientific interest in the supernatural and catching the attention of contemporary society has been the children of darkness—those involved in spiritism, witchcraft, the occult. As a report on exorcism by the former Anglican Bishop of Exeter (1972) points out:

> In Western countries today, the widespread apostasy from the Christian faith, accompanied by an increasing recourse to black magic and the occult practices, is revealing the presence and the power of evil forces. . . .[1]

Yet the scientists investigating the spirit realm fail to realize that when "scientific" study is made of these evil forces, the conclusions are *bound to be false*. Why? Because the "data" from which these conclusions are drawn is innately unreliable. How could it be otherwise when Satan is the father of lies and the master of deception? Only the Word of God and the Holy Spirit can bring to light the true nature and mode of operation of the sinister powers of this dark world.

Nevertheless, when those outside the Church became entranced with the supernatural power of evil, the Church came out of the closet and admitted that the devil is for real. When this word got around, Satan dipped into his second bag of tricks. Invariably, whenever he is exposed, he kicks up a fuss to draw attention away from God to himself.

Unfortunately, many sincere Christians play into his hand. Fascinated by his diabolical dramatics, some virtually swing a spotlight on Satan cavorting center stage. When this happens, a captive audience can become caught up with what is happening in the demon world. The tendency then is to give this realm far more attention than it needs and credit it with more power and influence than it really has.

Certainly casting out demons is the work of God through His Church. But the danger inherent in concentrating on casting out demons is spelled out in the psychological principle, "Whatever gets your attention gets you."

What's more, demonology has another inherent snag. It affords an *out* for those who tend to sidestep responsibility for their own deeds. Often it is not *deliverance* that is needed, but *self-discipline*. And even when deliverance is called for, sin must still be dealt with and self-discipline follow if the person is to remain free.

For those who neither fall for the lie that he doesn't exist nor get preoccupied with his antics, Satan resorts to his third bag of tricks. He can still score if he can convince Christians they are too smart or too spiritual to be deceived. This isn't difficult, human pride being what it is.

To be sure, everything needed to protect ourselves from the Enemy is ours in Christ—*if* we heed the warnings and obey the rules. But who takes action to protect himself from an enemy posing no threat?

In his outstanding book, *Deliver Us From Evil*, Anglican priest John Richards warns:

> Who are the casualties in warfare? The disobedient, the unarmed, the weak, the undisciplined, and those with illusions about the war being somewhere else! So too are the casualties in spiritual warfare.[2]

Being a Spirit-filled Christian does not make one immune to the devil's trickery. So it's crucial to shape up, spy out the Enemy's strategy, and give attention to the battle being waged. This means confronting the popular theologies of our day and scrutinizing them in the light of the Scriptures. When we do, we may be shocked to discover how many turn out to be not so biblical after all.

There is something else we need to face. The men and women

who initiate unscriptural theologies and practices are not guilty alone. To become popular, false teaching must be seized upon and eagerly spread by countless individuals. What's more, zealous Christians can thoughtlessly encourage false teaching.

For example, I think of one widely acclaimed healing evangelist some years back with an unusually gifted ministry. The time eventually came when he claimed to be Elijah incarnated.[3] He promised that if he died, he would come back to life three days later. Then he was killed in a grinding car crash. Until the government stepped in, his followers refused to let him be buried. They were waiting for him to be resurrected, according to the "new revelation" he had received.

I asked a friend who had known this evangelist through the years, "How could a man who once had such a valid ministry get so far off?"

"I blame the people," he said. "They were always pressing him to seek God for a *new* revelation. That is always dangerous."

Now I find myself asking, Has something similar been happening in the renewal movement?

To begin with, dead, dry Christianity was sparked to life with the fiery message that Jesus is Lord, that the Holy Spirit empowers believers to live subject to His lordship, and that the gifts of the Spirit are needed and available for today. These truths were translated into the personal experience of countless numbers of people. What happened was a sovereign move of the Spirit without form or fences. And it was exciting.

But some leaders caught up in the momentum and eager to prevent any slackening of enthusiasm spoke about *new* revelation. God, they said, had a *new* word for this hour. What followed underscores Paul's final words to Timothy:

> . . . For the time will come when men will not put up with sound doctrine. Instead, to suit their own desires, they will gather around them a great number of teachers to say *what their itching ears want to hear.* They will turn their ears away from the truth and turn aside to myths. But you, keep your head in all situations, *endure hardship.* . . .[4] (Emphasis mine.)

What are these *new* revelations which have become movements in themselves? Precisely what man's "itching ears" want to hear—surefire formulas to achieve health, wealth, success, happiness, and personal fulfillment. After all, few want to be reminded that Jesus said following Him is *costly*, and that the cost entails *persecution*, *pain*, and *personal loss*.

Yet the aged apostle warned Timothy not to fall for teaching that caters to one's comfort and encourages self-indulgence. "Join with me in suffering for the gospel,"[5] he challenged Timothy from prison. "Endure hardship."[6]

A good share of the popular contemporary theologies incur the deception Paul denounced so vigorously in Romans, chapter one: worshiping and serving the creature rather than the Creator. When that happens, instead of one's relationship to God having top priority, human relationships shift to the number-one place. And loving oneself outranks all other relationships.

There are other wrinkles. These fanciful and narrow interpretations of Scripture would have us manipulate God by praise, our husbands by sex, and if we are at the top of "the chain of command," control others by usurping "delegated authority."

Even submission has become self-serving—the means to finagle one's way out of making hard decisions or learning to know God's voice for oneself. And, sadly, where Christians once confidently affirmed, "The Lord is my shepherd," "new revelation" has left many wandering in a maze asking, "*Who is my shepherd?*"—until they blindly submit to some human authority, bow, and quakingly confess, "My shepherd is my lord"!

Furthermore, among these movements, secular humanism masquerades as various spiritual therapies designed to make us happy, authentic, fulfilled. Of course, these spiritual therapies are only secular therapies refurbished with religious terminology. Nothing wrong with that—except that they are death-producing if they substitute human endeavor for the need to confess and forsake one's sins and experience the transforming work of the Holy Spirit.

Without question, the gifts of the Spirit, miracles, and supernatural religious phenomena do occur when there is a genuine move of God. But there are some who dare to manipulate people to fake the real. Spiritual reality is thus obscured in a haze of hypocrisy.

Mind you, we need relevant teaching, biblical principles applied to present dilemmas of life. And it's right that we appreciate a demonstration of God's power. But when these things get distorted, and Christ is lost in the shadows, they become the devil's snare.

In writing his autobiography at eighty-three, E. Stanley Jones took the long-range look backward and said, "Christ has been, and is, to me the Event. . . . In his light I will try to see life."[7] As a young evangelist, Jones saw the danger of becoming sidetracked. He wrote:

> I once traveled during my formative evangelistic years with a very great man. I learned much from him. But when his emphasis shifted from Christ to varying emphases—antiwar programs, social justice, birth control, spiritualism—he was less than effective; he was a blur. He would exhaust these emphases in a year or two and have to shift to a new one. But you do not exhaust Christ—he is the inexhaustible. Events come and go; the Event remains unchanged amid the changeable.[8]

In our various approaches to relating biblical principles to particular human need, our main focus must always be "the Event"—the dynamic living Christ.

We pray, "Thy kingdom come, thy will be done on earth as it is in heaven." But the Bible tells us heaven pulsates with the sound of voices raised in worship of a *holy* God: "*Holy, holy, holy is the Lord God Almighty, who was, and is, and is to come.*"[9] When His will is done in us as it is in heaven, this likewise becomes our song on earth. A sense of God's holiness, like nothing else, will turn us back from egocentric theology to being Christocentric in doctrine and deed. It is with joy and anticipation, then, that we will from first to last embrace the Event.

When Jesus spoke of the narrow way which leads to life,[10] He was not talking about narrow-mindedness. Rather, the "narrow way" is the midline between two extremes, the built-in balance of biblical doctrine. Look at the Scriptures: Faith is balanced by works, God's love by His wrath, His mercy by His justice, man's responsibility by God's sovereignty, the role of royal sons by that of obedient servants, death to self by life in the Spirit. But in the fog that has enveloped the renewal and the Church at large, it is not always easy to find the narrow way. Not easy—but so necessary.

Where I grew up on the shore of Puget Sound, the fog would sometimes be so thick that standing in the door of Dad's station, one could not see the gas pumps a dozen feet away. If Charlie Skinner happened to be having his car worked on when the mists began moving in, he would leave his car and walk the two miles home. Charlie knew from dreadful experience the danger of driving when one cannot see clearly. Years before, in a pea-soup fog, he had careened off the road and rolled down an embankment. His wife was thrown out, and the car flipped over, killing her.

The danger is no less real on our spiritual journey when our perception is beclouded by fuzzy half-truths and murky renderings of Scripture. Surely it is time we let the light of God's Word and the breath of the Spirit penetrate and blow away the fog that has settled in to obscure the narrow way.

1

Following Jesus for Fun and Profit

Walking up the driveway, I flipped through the pile of slush mail and pulled out a fat envelope boldly stamped *Attention: Prosperity Packet Enclosed.* My blood pressure did a quick push-up. With Al's job at a Christian college involving far more dedication than remuneration, it wasn't that we couldn't use some prosperity. But I was sure that the sender's intent was not to ease our financial strain, but to finagle funds for some cause.

I was right. The packet proved to be a dozen Bible verses printed on 1″ x 2″ cards. The enclosed letter stated that they were God's promises that I should claim for prosperity. I was to carry them with me at all times, read them at every opportunity, say them aloud—and wait for the money to roll in. My contribution to the sender would be an act of faith which would begin releasing God's supply.

The prosperity packet was just another double-dealing device to obtain donations.

I remember when we used to chuckle at the radio evangelists who promised to reward contributors with an autographed picture. Today's appeals are much more sophisticated—and shocking. "Blessed" cloths, "blessed" burlap, "blessed" palm branches, "blessed" keys, "blessed" mustard seed, rice and cement for the sender to "bless" and return, new pennies, and even a silk handkerchief to wrap your problems in and return for prayer!

Even without the "blessed" enclosures, many appeals for funds, whether they come over the air or on the "personal" stationery of the solicitor, are nonetheless deceptive. And the deceit is swelled when letters are made to appear personal by inserting the addressee's name in every other paragraph. Sadly, this tactic actually convinces some people that they are receiving personal attention. The pat on their egos incites them to give—which is, of course, the sender's intent.

The biggest prosperity fraud is the promising of double returns, or more, on one's "faith gift" or "planted seed." Many have stampeded the bandwagon, but it is a bandwagon gone wild.

Years ago, my husband and I learned the hard way about this sort of propaganda. We had traveled a hundred miles to attend a healing campaign which drew crowds numbering in the thousands. At one meeting faith-promise pledges were solicited for the support of the organization during the coming year. One was all but guaranteed that the Lord would provide not only money to pay the pledge, but double that amount. Dramatic confirming testimonies were recounted.

Yes, we had been blessed by the preaching of the Word, and we had been impressed by what we had seen and felt in the services. Our faith was running high—we thought. But even if it wasn't adequate, the speaker reassured us, "You may not feel you have faith, but I will put your name on my faith-partner prayer list, and I will personally pray for you every day. I will believe God to meet your every need and bless you with twice as much as you give. I will use my faith . . . "

I nudged Al. "Let's make a pledge of two hundred dollars."

He frowned. "But how can we pay that much above what we are already giving?"

"You heard what he said. How can we lose? God has to supply, and He will bless us more in the end."

So we made the pledge. And though we prayed and scraped, we simply couldn't come up with the extra two hundred dollars. I think we may have ended up using our tithe to finish paying off our commitment.

What went wrong? Was it lack of faith? Admittedly, faith was lacking. And another thing—our motive was wrong. Still, what we did seemed right at the time because of who was presenting the appeal and the scripture he used to back it. The painful result of desperately trying to fulfill our obligation taught us to beware of this enticement. Never again, we agreed, would we fall for that line.

Was Paul Wrong?

But what about "giving to get"? Clearly the principle is found in the Bible. Jesus said to give and it shall be given. And Paul reminded the Corinthians, "Whoever sows sparingly will also reap sparingly, and whoever sows generously will also reap generously."[1] But is that all that Jesus and Paul had to say about Christian giving? If the project-promoters look at chapters 8 and 9 of 2 Corinthians for a plug from Paul, they will be disappointed. Paul did not talk about giving to *deserving projects* but to *destitute people*—the saints in need.

Because of their faith, the large community of Jerusalem Christians had become increasingly impoverished since being cut off from the non-Christian Jewish community. The break with relatives, with temple worship, and with the social structure had resulted in widespread unemployment and hardship. Now famine added to their distress.

Paul knew that the need was not merely material. The Christians in Jerusalem needed to realize the scope and unity of the Body of Christ—that they were not struggling alone. Also, the Gentile Christians needed to express loving concern in a tangible way for their Jewish brothers and sisters in Christ. Sending money would relieve the financial distress, and the act of love would strengthen the whole church and glorify God.

Earlier that year when Titus was in Corinth, a collection was started. Now Paul appealed to the Corinthians to follow through on their initial enthusiasm. To encourage their giving, he set forth two examples. The first, the Macedonian churches. Although the Macedonians were undergoing severe trial and extreme poverty, they gave far beyond what Paul had expected. Their outstanding generosity, he pointed out, was a demonstration of the grace of God. His second example was Christ. Foregoing His exalted position and turning His back on the wealth of heaven, Christ limited himself to a human body, becoming poor that they might become rich.

Along with his appeal, the Apostle gave some practical advice: Giving should be in proportion to one's means. God isn't so much concerned with the amount one gives as with his *willingness* to give. No one is to go into debt in order to give. Sharing was to make for equality—the ones who have providing for those who have not.

Further, Paul insisted that delegates be appointed by the churches to collect the money. He was determined not to give an occasion for anyone to say that he had mishandled these funds.

Paul's approach was quite different from the appeals which turn up in my mailbox. Though it was a tough situation for the Christians in Jerusalem, Paul said very little about their plight. No graphic pictures were painted of the hungry. No details of the destitute were described. Paul simply presented the need. He didn't want anyone to give out of false guilt. Sincere love would see sharing with the saints-in-need as a privilege. And giving would be the joyous and spontaneous response of those who confessed the gospel of Christ.

At the same time, Paul did present, as an incentive to giving, the principle of reaping what is sown. Certainly, then, it cannot be wrong to expect God's blessing when we give. But is God obligated to reward our giving with material abundance? Has He promised to make us wealthy?

He is! and He has! say heralds of the gospel of success. Anyone can and should believe and achieve . . . confess and possess . . . claim and obtain. . . . One is limited only by one's lack of faith. You can have anything if you believe it. So goes the pitch.

Many concerned Christians see this gospel of success as one of the most threatening deceptions to the Church today.

Foxes Have Holes, and Birds Have Nests, but . . .

How times have changed! One thing I knew as a growing child: Christian discipleship was costly. One gave up the *claim* to success, fame, and wealth. A common song of commitment was, "I Surrender All." Now I am told I can have the best of both worlds. The rags-to-riches prophets dangle the promise of material blessings as an enticement to follow Christ, and prosperity as the birthright of all Christians.

But are riches the lure that Jesus used when He called men and women to follow Him? Treasures in heaven—yes; treasures on earth—no.

Jesus laid down some tough requirements for discipleship. To the man who said he would follow Jesus wherever He went, Jesus said nothing about *profit*. He talked about *cost*. Foxes have holes, and birds have nests, Jesus said, but He had no place to lay His head, no home on earth to call His own. Following Jesus meant a life of insecurity—if one needed material things in order to be secure.

Another would-be disciple heard Christ's call and said he'd follow as soon as he buried his father and said good-bye to his family. But it was probably his inheritance he wanted to secure. Since burials had to take place within twenty-four hours of death, it seemed highly unlikely that the father was already dead. In order to claim his legacy the son would have to remain at home until the father died—then he could follow Jesus.

But that wouldn't work. "No one who puts his hand to the plow and looks back is fit for service in the kingdom of God,"[2] said Jesus. The business of the kingdom was much too pressing to delay. Personal resources were not necessary for discipleship. In fact, *any* hindrance to carrying out one's commitment to follow Jesus had to be given up.

Silver and Gold Have I None?

One of the most prominent features of the renewal during the early sixties was the remarkable stories of God intervening in the business affairs of believers. The dominant theme of many meetings and magazines was how God had filled men and women with the Holy Spirit and subsequently blessed them financially. The attraction was tremendous; God was revealed to many in a *new* way—as a loving Father concerned about every aspect of their lives.

But as time went on, the success testimonials gave the impression of having turned into the game, "Can you top that?" To one who didn't know better, the Spirit-filled life might have seemed an open sesame to Fort Knox. The success syndrome characterized more and more of the renewal preaching, and the following of the prosperity teaching grew.

This gilded thinking was not new to me. Some years before, we had friends who helped in the outreach at a skid-row mission. We wouldn't have called them wealthy, but the woman did have a fur coat. In those days, a fur coat was definitely a status symbol. Because those who stumbled into the mission were wretchedly poor, one day someone questioned the appropriateness of the wife's wearing her fur coat at the mission.

"Oh," she said, "I tell the poor people that if they follow Jesus and pay their tithe, they can have a fur coat too."

But does anyone have a right to make such a promise?

The Bible does say, "Bring ye all the tithes into the storehouse . . . and prove me . . . if I will not open you the windows of heaven, and pour you out a blessing, that there shall not be room enough to receive it."[3] But is the promised "overflow blessing" to consist of fur coats, diamonds, palatial houses, and Lincoln Continentals?

Old Testament scripture depicts God's blessing on Israel to be directly related to the number of a man's sons, and to the size of his flocks and herds. New Testament saints are more often depicted as robed in adversity. Even those who started out rich ended up poor.

Take Peter, James, and John. First they left *all* to follow Jesus. Then they ended up among those believers in the Early Church who had all things in common, sharing all their possessions.

If giving always pays off in material gain, Peter, James, and John should have become millionaires and more. But when Peter and John met the blind beggar at the Beautiful Gate, Peter told him, "Silver or gold I do not have."[4] Nor did John reach for his wallet.

Neither did James identify with the affluent, but he had a word for them: "Now listen, you rich people. . . . Your wealth has rotted. . . . Your gold and silver are corroded. Their corrosion will testify against you. . . . You have hoarded wealth in the last

days. . . . You have lived on earth in luxury and self-indulgence."⁵

For that matter, in spite of the deluge of promises of prosperity for the obedient, the good fortune of the wicked was a sore
point to more than one Old Testament traveler of faith. The
truth is that throughout the Bible, monuments to faith are built
of the glorious—and the gory. (If you don't think so, read Jeremiah and Hebrews 11:35-38.)

If material blessing were in direct proportion to one's giving
or one's faith, wealth would be a slide rule for measuring spirituality. But if we attempt to use such a gauge, we come up with
some staggering contradictions. Paul for one. There were times
when he lived in plenty, but at the time he wrote First Corinthians, he said of himself and Apollos, "To this very hour we go
hungry and thirsty, we are in rags, we are brutally treated, we are
homeless."⁶ And, it is on this note that he reminded the Corinthians that he was their spiritual father, and said, "I urge you to
imitate me . . . my way of life in Christ Jesus, which agrees with
what I teach everywhere in every church."⁷

Still, this is the same Paul who also told the Corinthians, "If
you sow generously, 'you will be made rich in every way.' "⁸

So what are we to think?

Christians must realize there is a tension between the *cost*
and the *blessing* spiritual and economic of following Jesus
which cannot be resolved by emphasizing the cost and denouncing the blessing. Or conversely, by emphasizing the blessing and
denouncing the cost.

Unfortunately, the Church has seen the exaltation of both extremes. Early Christianity was heavily imprinted by the rigorous
ascetics, and by the Church fathers who vigorously attacked luxury and held poverty to be an important Christian virtue. The intense pursuit of the *De Imitatione Christi* was expressed by self-
inflicted austerity. Monasticism developed out of the notion that
Christians must detach themselves from the world to perfect
their holiness.

Quite unlike the Early Church, the contemporary church has
sprouted a philosophy of the opposite extreme. Christ's death, we
are told, "became our 'deed' to all the elements of royalty—

especially health and wealth.''[9] God's hands are filled with dollars and diamonds for His kids—He never meant them for the devil's offspring. So, release your faith and help yourself!

Had anyone dared voice such thoughts to the Early Church fathers, I can see the shocked faces and hear the shouts of heresy.

As it happens, a growing number of Christians today are registering shock and disapproval over the current stress on material blessing. They recognize that the doctrine that equates redemption with rags-to-riches is seeded with deception. But neither does the Bible teach that poverty is synonymous with spirituality. Either extreme is Satan's underhanded push to distort the biblical perspectives of the cost and the blessing of following Jesus. Balance is needed. I find no warnings in the Bible against those who teach self-denial of this world's goods, but it is full of warnings against those who teach that "godliness is a means to financial gain."[10] Perhaps this is because wealth is far more enticing than poverty.

No doubt it will be argued that the issue is not one of either riches or God—but it is both riches and God, and in any event God is given the glory. What comes through loudest, however, is not God's benevolent sovereignty, but rather man's faith, cleverness, motivation, and ability to apply success principles to whatever he does.

Give to, or Take from, the Poor?

A paramount problem with the gospel of success is that it is the product of the Western mind, oriented to Western ideology and culture. Try to apply it to situations around the world and the success-prosperity pitch becomes glaringly absurd.

Imagine Mother Teresa stooping over a dying beggar sprawled in the mud- and dung-filled streets in India to inform him God wants him to be rich in this world's goods.

Or take the families which make up the underground church in Russia. The lives and witness of these believers depend very much on their keeping a low profile. If God were to suddenly "bless" them with an affluent life-style, what would happen?

Let the pictures roll: A soldier sloshing through a steamy

jungle. A starving Cambodian mother, her infant pulling at her dry breast. A Jew or an Arab dazedly picking through the ruins of what was his dwelling before the bombs fell. A murderer slumped in the corner of his cell on death row. A shriveled little grandmother dumped in a substandard nursing home. A mentally handicapped young man doing token work in a community shelter . . .

What about these very real limitations? Is it not irresponsible and irrational to preach that faith in Christ makes us here-and-now inheritors of this world's riches? Is it not a shame to preach that whether or not a person receives this inheritance, which is declared to be paid for by Christ's death, depends solely on the person's *willingness* to live in divine prosperity? Or, as some preach, that giving guarantees a lucrative return? True, the limitations are not of God. Nevertheless, they do exist. And in view of these limitations, does anyone have the right to embellish the message of salvation with the universal promise of prosperity?

The memory still haunts me of a young woman who came forward for prayer at a convention banquet some years ago. The problem, she tearfully told me, was financial. Complicated circumstances and a series of calamities left her and her husband hard pressed to provide the family's most basic needs. During this time they had been urged by other Christians to give away what little they did have so God would provide more. Having given away the remainder, there was nothing left. They were in the worst straits imaginable. What should they do?

The minister standing beside me bobbed his head. "Just start giving, sister . . ."

I cut in. "But she says that is what they have done." Certainly he couldn't have heard what the woman said! By now she was sobbing heavily.

But the preacher gave me a look that indicated it was all settled, and said, "Just keep giving." With that he walked away.

I mumbled something. Then I turned aside to pray with someone else, but I felt like a traitor. That desperate young mother came to us for help, and what she received was cottony words.

Looking back, I don't feel quite so guilty. I don't think the answer was to be found in prayer at the meeting. Help should have been forthcoming from her church. Not only dollars-and-cents help, but the counsel of someone skilled in finance who could have helped untangle the mess and advise the woman and her husband wisely in future money matters.

Strange, isn't it, how "spiritual" solutions are preferred to the "practical" by so many Christians.

And here's a clincher. Had Paul taken this single approach—giving to get—to the needs at Jerusalem, he would not have told the churches at Macedonia, Galatia, and Corinth to send aid to their fellow Christians. Rather, he would have told the Jerusalem believers to start giving out of their poverty and God would see that their purses were soon bulging!

Another thing. If giving—or faith alone, or the two together—can get us anything we ask for, then those who say so should be the world's greatest philanthropists. Instead of using faith-success principles to get more and more things for themselves, why don't they apply them to provide the good life for Christian brothers and sisters in the Third World, or for those mired in the ghettos of poverty here in the United States? After all, the Bible says, "Do good to all people, especially to those who belong to the family of believers."[11]

We have to ask why the God-wants-you-rich prophets don't take their message where it is needed most. Compared to millions around the world, the persons to whom they address themselves are already wealthy. But they shrug and say, "Wealth is relative, of course, a matter of degree. And we have needs in our culture that others don't have."

But you and I need to remember that not all the King's kids are dressed in suits and ties, or fancy dresses, or designer jeans. This very hour, brothers and sisters in Christ are suffering deprivation, torture, and even martyrdom. Considering this, I cringe whenever a church leader who lives in unrestrained luxury says that prosperity is God's stamp of approval on his life and work!

Jesus laid it on the line. It is hard for a rich man to enter the kingdom of heaven because money does not usually serve people, people usually serve money. And Jesus said, "You cannot serve both God and Money."[12]

Paul zeros in on what can happen when one hankers after wealth. "People who want to get rich [not who *are rich*, but who *want to get rich*] fall into temptation and a trap and into many foolish and harmful desires that plunge men into ruin and destruction."[13] He mourned the tragic consequences for those who, "eager for money, have wandered from the faith and pierced themselves with many griefs."[14]

Long before Paul's time, Agur, penning Proverbs 30, spelled out the danger explicitly. Here we find a man awed by the immensity of God. Longing to know God, he readily admits his inability to understand God's majesty and power.

Yet Agur knows two things about God: *"Every word of God is flawless,"* and *"He is a shield to those who take refuge in him."*[15]

At the same time, Agur is quick to realize that certain circumstances could alter his attitude toward God. His concern is that this not happen. Listen to his prayer:

"Two things I ask of you, O Lord;
  do not refuse me before I die:
Keep falsehood and lies far from me;
  give me neither poverty nor riches,
  but give me only my daily bread.
Otherwise, I may have too much and disown you
  and say, 'Who is the Lord?'
Or I may become poor and steal,
  and so dishonor the name of my God."[16] (Emphasis mine.)

Agur's plea is amazingly relevant! "Lord, don't let me even get near anyone peddling the lie that poverty is a virtue, or promoting the fallacy that God wants me rich." He saw the imminent danger of both poverty and affluence. Poverty, because it might push him to stealing and so to dishonoring God's name. Riches, because he might lose the wonder of God and think that he did it on his own and no longer needed God.

This very perceptive man asks only that his daily needs be met, no stockpile, no accumulated wealth. And the rightness of his request is affirmed by the prayer Jesus taught His disciples when He said, "Give us today our daily bread."[17]

It comes down to this: We like to think it can't happen to us, but the more riches pile up, the more they tend to dim one's view of the Lord of Lords. To varying degrees, the rich often become little lords, using the power and prestige associated with wealth to build and control their little kingdom.

It is crucial that we hear Jesus say again and again, "Give to the poor." If we refuse to hear and obey, we will be spiritually the poorest of the poor.

What Do I Really Need?

It is one thing to be blessed with wealth, to recognize that all one has is from God, and to be a righteous steward of those blessings. It is quite another to hold the attitude, "I have a right to be rich!" Moreover, when someone defends an indulgent life-style, a look behind the scenes may reveal that accumulated wealth is often at the expense of the less fortunate.

Some months ago I was having dinner with a couple, prominent promoters of the gospel of success. When the waitress handed me the menu, the husband said, "Order anything you like. Nothing is too good for the King's kids." The catch was, I knew this couple's business was in trouble, their bills were not being paid, and many of the people to whom they owed money were hurting financially. I would have felt much more comfortable eating at McDonald's.

Unscrupulous business tactics and oppression of the poor by the rich were recurrent themes of Old Testament prophets. The prophets didn't mince words as to what God thought of such action. We have no reason to believe God has changed His mind.

Admittedly, we can pull certain verses out of context and buttress a rags-to-riches doctrine. For instance, someone takes Paul's statement, "You will be made rich in every way,"[18] and says, "Hey! God wants me to have a superabundance of this world's goods!" But if we listen carefully to *all* that Paul said, we know he had something quite different in mind than mere material blessing. We can outline his points this way:

If you give generously and joyfully:

1. God will be pleased.
2. God is able to make all grace abound to you.
   You will have all that you need.
   God will increase what you are able to give

        by making what you have left over go farther than it
would otherwise.

        by making you rich in every way so you can be generous on every occasion.

3. You will prove yourselves sincere in your love, not by how much you have, but by how much you share with those in need.

4. Many will give thanks to God
        for His grace to you.
        for His indescribable Gift!

No question about it, God does promise to supply everything we need. But often our trouble is in discerning what is essential. I love the story told by Bill Pethybridge of the Worldwide Evangelization Crusade. He was to speak at a church on the other side of London and had only enough money for carfare there—not back. He went, believing God would supply the return fare at the other end.

After the service he lingered, chatting, thinking someone would slip him a shilling—maybe even invite him for a meal. But one after another said thanks for coming and good-bye. Finally he was standing all alone. "But, Lord," he groaned, "You promised to supply all my needs."

"Yes, I did," the Lord said, "and you need exercise. Start walking!"

Through the years, Al and I have marveled again and again at how God has met our needs. One particular time stands out because we saw God monitoring our needs even before we were aware of an upcoming need.

One night at Bible school, when we came back to our room, there was a plain envelope marked, "Florence," on my desk. Inside was a five-dollar bill. It was the only time during our three years in Bible school that such a gift had showed up designated specifically for *me*. I slipped the money into my empty wallet.

The next afternoon Al was involved in a serious explosion at work. When I first saw him, they were bringing him up from Emergency to ICU. His left hand and forearm were horribly burned, and he was in critical condition with a brain concussion.

I would be staying at the hospital with him and I needed money for meals and for phone calls to our families. Twenty-four hours earlier, we didn't have a cent. But when the need arose, God had already supplied.

God has supplied our needs in extraordinary and ordinary ways more times than I can begin to recount. Paul was right. God has fantastic ways to make what we have go further than it would otherwise.

Still, I suspect there have been times when God wanted to stretch our faith to believe, but we failed and were the poorer for it. A prayer I pray over and over is, "Lord, help me to learn how to receive what You want me to have."

Spiritual Blessings/Financial Blessings

If you ask a Christian why God doesn't prosper all His children financially, you will probably receive one of two answers. The most frequent, "Because He can't trust everybody with money." The other, "Lack of faith!"

But is it really that simple? What *was* the overflow blessing Malachi promised? And what did Jesus have in mind when He said, "Give, and it will be given to you. A good measure, pressed down, shaken together and running over, will be poured into your lap. For with the measure you use, it will be measured to you"?[19]

Malachi wrote, "Thus saith the Lord: 'I will open you the windows of *heaven*. . . .' " Evidently the blessing He has promised to pour out is in the *spiritual* realm—no matter what the material results may be.

When God throws open the windows of heaven, the sunlight of His love streams forth. There is fresh air to replace the air that has become stale from our dwelling in the limited confines of the self-life. No longer are our prayers centered around, "Lord, bless me!" Instead, we give and pray, "Lord, bless others!" And because our praying is accompanied by giving, our prayers have a greater impact; we really believe in the thing we are praying for.

Through giving—our tithe is but a part—we discover a new spiritual freedom. We think in new dimensions. By giving, we "enlarge the place of [our] tent."[20]

Since money is a token of our labor, when we give it we give a part of ourselves—our time and energy. A gift to the poor is an investment of ourselves in the lives of men and women, boys and girls. Money given to support missionaries also enables us to extend ourselves far beyond the circle of self.

Giving makes us stockholders in the kingdom of God, where we have an unlimited outreach. Through responsible giving, our hands are extended to those we could touch in no other way.

Giving enriches our perception of the Body of Christ and ourselves as a part of that body. Sharing our finances with our brothers and sisters in need is sharing ourselves. Although giving is not what makes us a part of the Body of Christ, our giving enables the body to function at its greatest capacity. The Body of Christ is potentially limitless in its bounds and accomplishments!

Is it any wonder God speaks of a blessing "that there shall not be room enough to receive it"?

When Ken and Bess Adams opened a Christian bookstore in a little village in England, they started their enterprise on a borrowed 100 pounds ($300) made available by extraordinary means. Beginning in two small upstairs rooms, their bookstore grew until they felt impressed to give their business to the Lord. Not just 10 percent—but *all*.

After much prayer, they did just that.

Her voice surging with the thrill of what God has done, Bess Adams told me, "This is the real tithe. We chose to give it to the Lord that He might bless and multiply. Like Paul, we could then say, 'As poor, yet making many rich; as having nothing, and yet possessing all things.' "[21]

"As far as prospering financially," she laughed, "I still praise the Lord when I receive a dollar. But you see, the invisible blessings are always greater than the visible. We are poor, but because we gave our *all* to Him, He has enabled us to 'make many rich' by giving them the gospel."

Out of these small beginnings in 1941 came the Christian Literature Crusade which has grown to a team of almost 600 men and women, serving in 47 countries and sending the printed message into another 100 countries. Over 150 bookcenters in strategic cities serve as bases of operation for distributing literature in over 75 languages.

Thus the Lord truly opened the windows of heaven, and Ken and Bess Adams found that the blessing He poured out could not be contained.

What was the good measure "pressed down, shaken together and running over" Jesus said would be given to us according to what we give? Was it money and things we associate with the good life?

No. Jesus was talking about loving our enemies, forgiveness, extending mercy. "Then your reward will be great, and you will be sons of the Most High. . . . Be merciful, just as your Father is merciful,"[22] He said.

Two things occur to me. First, you and I desperately need mercy "pressed down, shaken together and running over." So we had better give mercy—lavishly. The other, if God in mercy did not *withhold* many things we ask in prayer, we would certainly have long ago destroyed ourselves. After all, if Eve hadn't wanted more than God's provision, she wouldn't have gotten herself into such a mess.

Like Abraham, we need to know experientially that God is *El-Shaddai*—the Almighty, the *God-who-is-enough*.[23] Jesus says it is wrong to worry about what we will eat or wear; if He can feed the birds and dress the lilies in such wondrous garb, He can certainly "much more" provide our temporal needs. Our job is to "seek first his kingdom and his righteousness."[24] "All these things" will then be ours as well.

"The pagans run after all these things"[25]—the temporal and the transient. But why should we? Our heavenly Father knows our need and will supply.

Name It, Claim It!

What about the teaching that we can have anything we ask for in faith? Are there—or are there not—limitations to what God will do in answer to our prayers?

Not only are financial problems due to lack of faith, say the prosperity hucksters, but so is sickness. I still get the chills when I recall a dinner that I sat through prior to speaking. A man at the table fiercely denounced a minister who is known for an extremely sacrificial, compassionate, and fruitful ministry. "Calls himself a man of God," he sneered. "He's no man of God; his wife has cancer! He needs to get it straight from ————" (and he named two leading exponents of the heavy guilt-producing teaching that if one is sick the fault is one's own lack of faith).

Since the Bible directs us to bear one another's burdens, I wondered what prevented this man from speaking the needed word of faith to bring healing to the minister's wife. How dare he shift the blame if he truly believed faith always guarantees healing!

One wonders, too, how much spiritual agony has been caused by the "name it, claim it" advocates. Faithful saints suffering and in pain are tormented with the accusation that if they only believed, Jesus would heal them. When they're not healed, they feel guilty. Family and friends are also racked with false guilt. Meanwhile, Mr. Name-it-claim-it, feeling quite smug about his distinguished spiritual ministry, hurries off to spread his destructive influence elsewhere.

It may startle you to learn that Jesus' prayers were not always answered—not when He wept (the Greek word is literally *sobbed* or *wailed loudly*) over Jerusalem. He wanted so much for those within her walls to know peace and righteousness. He would have gathered the people, like a hen does her chicks, to himself—but they would not. The final decision rested with each man and woman.

Neither did Paul always receive his requests. The thorn in his flesh wasn't removed.[26] And Demas, "because he loved this world," and Phygelus and Hermogenes and "everyone in the province of Asia" deserted Paul. Surely Paul and Luke must have had intense prayer sessions for their fellow workers and for the believers in Asia. But it didn't change the course these individuals set themselves to follow.

Can my prayer save a lost person against his or her will? The Bible says that each person is ultimately responsible for his eternal destiny. Can we wipe out poverty with our prayers? Jesus said the poor will always be with us. Nevertheless, prayer is the awesome responsibility of every Christian. It is difficult to understand why, but God has deliberately chosen to limit himself, in a tremendous measure, to the prayers of His people.

Success and Failure

The other paraprosperity doctrine says, "God won't let me fail."

Here again we see the limited perspective most of us have. God looks at success and failure in the light of eternity. I've heard more than one minister say that the utter failure he experienced in one pastorate proved to be the best thing that had ever happened to him. What if success means men and women get so caught up in their business and careers that God is pushed to the fringes? Failure—if it happens—may well be a blessing.

Sometimes it takes failure to drive us to a deeper commitment than we would otherwise make. And sometimes failure serves as the motivation for us to get our priorities in line with God's. Failure is often God's discipline to keep us from going astray.

Who's Serving Whom?

Now considering all these things, and going back to Paul's principles for giving, we find our perspective on prosperity begins to clear. We see the biblical emphasis is not on giving to get for ourselves. The emphasis is not faith to get—but faith to give!

What's more, it is not what you and I give, but what we have left over that Jesus appraises. That is why the widow's mite was so special to Him.

Our motives and desires must, therefore, be transformed by the Spirit of God. Success prophets like to quote David's words, "Delight yourself in the Lord and he will give you the desires of your heart."[27] But the desires the Lord gives are *the desires that come from delighting in Him*. Besides, almost in the next breath, David concluded, "Better the little that the righteous have than the wealth of many wicked; for the power of the wicked will be broken, but the Lord upholds the righteous."[28]

Paul never lets us forget that true wealth is not this world's goods, but that in "godliness with contentment is great gain."[29]

This does not mean that God cannot change the economic condition of the poor, nor that He does not want to. It does not mean that Christians needn't work to bring about social and economic justice as much as possible.

It is very significant that the Christians I know who are deeply involved in responsible prison ministries, who are helping blacks to help themselves, who are working in drug and alcoholic rehabilitation programs, have not jumped on the gilded bandwagon. They are so taken up with giving, they have little time for an indulgent life-style.

It is true that one cannot give what one does not have. This is why Paul makes sure the Corinthians do not see God's material blessing as an end in itself. The whole idea behind God's enriching them in every way was so that they would have more to give. And the result of their generosity would be praise and thanksgiving to God for His indescribable gift.

The deception in the success-prosperity doctrine is subtle. It sounds so spiritual to assert that we cannot be sick or fail if we trust God, and that He will reward us for faith and giving and being good by making us rich in material things. But this was not the message of the Early Church fathers. Nor was it the message of the men and women of faith who throughout history set church and nation aflame with revival.

The more we pursue such poppycock, the more likely we will end up like pampered children. Getting everything we want won't turn us into soldiers for Christ. We may wear a tailored suit with gold buttons and hash marks, but we will be no more soldiers than the six-year-old with his feet shoved in his dad's old combat boots and carrying a wooden gun. Unchecked, the prosperity-success syndrome will not see Christians developing together into a vigorous, stouthearted, indomitable Church. Rather, it will reduce the Body of Christ to spiritual flabbiness.

The late Dr. A. W. Tozer, noted for his straightforward appeals for Christlike living, wrote:

> It seems that Christian believers have been going through a process of indoctrination and brainwashing, so it has become easy for us to adopt a kind of creed that makes God to be our servant instead of our being God's servant.
> Why should a man write and distribute a tract instructing us on "How to Pray so God Will Send You the Money You Need"?

Any of us who have experienced a life and ministry of faith can tell how the Lord has met our needs. My wife and I would probably have starved in those early years of ministry if we couldn't have trusted God completely for food and everything else. Of course, we believe that God can send money to His believing children—but it becomes a pretty cheap thing to get excited about the money and fail to give the glory to Him who is the Giver!

So many are busy "using" God. Use God to get a job. Use God to give us safety. Use God to give us peace of mind. Use God to obtain success in business. Use God to provide heaven at last.

Brethren, we ought to learn—and learn it very soon—that it is much better to have God first and have God Himself even if we have only a thin dime than to have all the riches and all the influence in the world and not have God with it![30]

Any time Satan can get us to shift our focus from the transcendent sovereignty and glory of the Holy One to "What's in it for me?" no matter how much of this world's goods we acquire, Satan is the one who benefits most.

It is our self-centered hankering for bigger and better, along with our cocky notion that God owes us anything we want, that makes us such an easy mark for most of Satan's propaganda.

2

Praise God for Everything?

Even though the Bible warns, "Do not go beyond what is written,"[1] men do. When valid biblical principles are extended beyond what God intended, the effects are disastrous. These effects can be understood in terms of Newton's universal law of motion: *Under the action of an external force, acceleration of a body occurs in proportion to the force.* Spiritually applied, the law of motion can be stated thus: the more dynamic the biblical principle, the more destructive its distortion.

No wonder Satan has been so keen on distorting the principle of praise! And no wonder the teaching of these distorted concepts has had such a sensational spread.

For many, praise has become nothing more than a fetish. A fetish is an object believed to have magical powers, or anything held in unreasoning devotion—exactly the sweeping sentiment regarding praise. Many among both the charismatics and the non-charismatics have taken praise as a panacea, a cure for every problem.

I know that God's Word abounds with exhortations to praise. What is more, we are not given an option; we are commanded to "give thanks in *all* circumstances"[2] and "for *all* things."[3]

But does this mean we are to thank and praise God for *sin*? Some teachers say we should.

When I first encountered this teaching, I immediately thought of Isaiah's thundering indictment, "Woe to those who call evil good!"[4] I thought, too, of Amos denouncing the nation of Israel because the people did not *grieve* over their sin. The cry of the prophet's heart was for repentance. God's people should not only "love good," but *"hate* evil." Any other attitude toward sin clashes with God's Word spoken through the Old Testament prophets.

Then I thought of Jesus. I could see Him on a dark, lonely night looking down on the flickering lights of Jerusalem, sobbing out the anguish of His heart, not praising God for the religious sterility of the Jewish leaders. Not praising God for the sin, the moral corruption within the city's gates, but weeping!

I thought of Jesus teaching His disciples to pray. "Affirm God's eternal kingdom, power, and glory," He said. "But when it comes to sin, pray to be kept from temptation and the Evil One."

I thought, too, of Paul. Did he praise God for the sexual immorality in the Corinthian church? Not for a moment! Instead, he wrote "out of great distress and anguish of heart and with many tears . . ."[5] that they might repent.

In fact, searching through the Scriptures, I could not find a single instance where men of faith offered thanks to God for sin. I am convinced that praising God for sin is not only unscriptural, but, in the light of Calvary, it is an appalling affront to God. If we offer praise to God for sin, we completely misunderstand the heart of God and His holiness.

In the light of Calvary, how can we praise God for our sin when our sin drove the spikes through the hands and feet and plunged the spear deep into the side of God's beloved Son? How can we thank God for sin when a holy God could not even look on the dark horror of sin laid on His sinless Son? How dare we offer praise for sin when sin caused that wrenching cry from the Savior's lips, "My God, my God, why have you forsaken me?"[6]

In the light of Calvary, I saw it clearly: praising God for sin puts us on the devil's side. Once we are on the devil's side, we begin thinking the devil's thoughts. Sin, rather than righteousness, becomes the accepted norm. *And the very sin for which we give thanks may shortly be our own undoing.*

Is it any wonder that at the same time the Church has been applauding this distorted teaching on praise, that divorce within the church family has become rampant? That divorce is almost an epidemic among the ministry?*

Personal Results of Praising God for Sin

I think of the minister whose writings tell how he prayed with a brokenhearted young man whose wife had left him. At the minister's urging, they knelt together and gave thanks that the wife was sleeping with another man.

When I read this, I was struck with a sense of outrage. At the same time, I could have wept. The minister was lining up on the devil's side and causing this young man to join him. Not long after reading this book I heard that the minister was involved in the breakup of two marriages, divorcing his wife to marry another.

I am not suggesting that this was the only reason behind this case of infidelity, divorce, and remarriage. But I am saying that whenever we are fooled into responding to any sin with praise and thanksgiving, our moral senses become dulled to the dreadfulness of that sin. This effects a breakdown of our moral defense. It follows, then, if we give praise for another's sexual immorality, stumbling into adultery will be easier than we would have ever thought. We are deceiving ourselves if we think that we are immune to this danger.

Then there is the effect upon our children. What young man, having known parental instruction in clean, moral living, would not be confused hearing Mom and Dad thank the Lord for a friend committing rape? Or what about the thirteen-year-old girl who hears her parents thank God that her sixteen-year-old sister has run away and is living with her boyfriend? As one thinking teenager said to me, "That wouldn't only cause confusion, it would cause rebellion!"

---

*Some argue that it is no different if a minister falls into sin than anyone else. But Jesus said, "From everyone who has been given much, much will be demanded; and from the one who has been entrusted with much, much more will be asked" (Luke 12:48). Both the Old Testament and the New Testament place greater responsibility on the leadership to live above reproach. When a leader is involved in divorce, others tend to rationalize their right to divorce also and follow suit. See: 2 Cor. 6:3 ff.; 1 Cor. 9:12; 1 Tim. 3:1-13; Titus 1:7-14; Lev. 21:22; Jer. 23:14 ff.

I saw a classic example of how sinister this teaching can be when I received a letter from Gini. She wrote:

> I've been reading a book that says we are to praise God for everything. I didn't think I could ever praise Him for being a homosexual. I couldn't even say the word. But finally, after a long struggle, I was able to say, "I am a homosexual." It hurt, but I immediately felt relief. Later I just poured out my heart to God—I thanked and praised Him that I am a homosexual. *If that's what He wanted for me, then I would have to accept it.* I also made up my mind never to practice it in actuality. The mind takes a little working on, but that's coming. (Emphasis mine.)

In the months since I had first met Gini, I had seen God bringing her out of darkness. She'd come a long way, but now this. She was thoroughly persuaded she should praise God for what He so vigorously condemns.

I tried to get Gini to see that verbally admitting she was a homosexual *was* important. Saying she was a homosexual, however, was not like saying she was female. Being female was essential to her being, her biological identity. Her choice had nothing to do with it.

On the other hand, being homosexual was neither essential to her being, nor a permanent identity rooted in her physical make-up. Being a homosexual was a matter of choice. She couldn't blame her behavior on God.

Persuaded to thank and praise the Lord that she was a homosexual, she presumed that this was her God-given form of human sexuality. But this is not what God wants—for her or anyone else. Accepting this special kind of mistaken identity, one of *being* rather than *doing*, and then thanking God for this evil, did not result in the spiritual strengthening she had expected. Instead, it was morally weakening, and it championed the devil's cause in her life.

The same sort of diabolical rending of Scripture by praisers-for-sin is common among "gay Christians." Passages which the Christian Church points to as condemning homosexual practices are used to argue the rightness of their life-style.

Take Romans 1:26, 27, the biblical passage most often quoted in reference to homosexuality. "Gay Christians" contend that

Paul is not saying here that homosexuality itself is sinful, but rather that it is a punishment for sin. The gays say, "Since 'God gave them up' to the homosexual condition as punishment for their sinful nature, . . . *the only godly response possible is to endure the chastening of the Lord with a joyful spirit.*"[7] (Emphasis mine.)

But the Apostle Paul's remarks on the matter are hardly conducive to joy. Rather, an alarm is sounded which needs to be heard by both the gays and those who would praise for this sin. The depravity of man, Paul declares, is not only evidenced in those who practice perversion, but also in those who *approve* of such evil (Rom. 1:32).

I can hear the praisers-for-sin protesting that praising does not mean they approve of the sin. But psychologically, this dichotomy is impossible. We simply are not able to render praise for sin and at the same time obey the scriptural injunction to "hate evil." This would be the ultimate "double-mindedness."[8]

And this, of course, is what Gini was trying to do. On the one hand, she was thanking and praising God and accepting homosexuality as being from Him. On the other, she was saying she couldn't "practice it in actuality," because God condemns it as sin.

If a man decides to drive his car in two opposite directions down the highway at once, he is going to spin out of control. It is inevitable. This is comparable to what Gini was doing when she attempted to commit herself, simultaneously, to two opposite positions. She was headed for a crash, which—when it came—was awful.

But what about the immediate relief Gini felt when she was finally able to say, "I am a homosexual"? Get whatever a person has been unwilling to face out in the open, say psychiatrists, and it will alleviate their internal conflict. But experience proves that while admitting the truth about ourselves does relieve feelings of anxiety and guilt, the relief is not necessarily enduring, especially if sin is involved. Only when we go through "God's therapeutic process" are these conflicts resolved with lasting results.

Only Jesus Christ can offer forgiveness and cleansing. And where we have been unable of ourselves to overcome an enslaving sin, He enables us through the power of His Holy Spirit to live free of its entrapment.

If Gini wanted to achieve this end, she would first of all have to put herself wholly on God's side. She would have to stop defending herself and start calling sin sin. She would have to line up with God against the lie that one cannot escape his homosexual orientation—no matter how many extenuating circumstances contribute to the deviancy. God's Word is very clear: "The reason the Son of God appeared was to destroy the devil's work."[9] *No matter what sin holds a person prisoner, a pardon is available, sealed with the precious blood of Jesus Christ.* The Bible promises, "If anyone is in Christ, he is a new creation."[10] Unless we insist on remaining locked up, bound by sin, the truth is, in Jesus Christ we are free. We have God's Word, infallible and irrefutable:

> Some sat in darkness and the deepest gloom,
>   prisoners suffering in iron chains,
> for they had rebelled against the words of God
>   and despised the counsel of the Most High. . . .
> Then they cried to the Lord in their trouble,
>   and he saved them from their distress.
> He brought them out of darkness and the deepest gloom
>   and broke away their chains.
> Let them give thanks to the Lord for his unfailing love
>   and his wonderful deeds for men,
> for he breaks down gates of bronze
>   and cuts through bars of iron.[11]

What Do We Give Thanks For?

The question still comes up, didn't Paul call upon us to give thanks for *all* things? Yes! he did. This bothered me until I found myself asking, "What does *thanks* imply?" And the obvious answer is, *a gift.* According to Webster, *thanks* is "the grateful acknowledgement of something received by or done for one."

So we can infer that "always giving thanks to God the Father for everything, in the name of our Lord Jesus Christ,"[12] means giving thanks for everything *God has given* us.

But God has not given us sin! Of this, we can be absolutely certain.

> For everything in the world—the cravings of sinful man, the lust of his eyes and the boasting of what he has and does—comes not from the Father but from the world.[13]
>
> When tempted, no one should say, "God is tempting me." For God cannot be tempted by evil, nor does he tempt anyone; but each one is tempted when, by his own evil desire, he is dragged away and enticed. Then, after desire has conceived, it gives birth to sin; and sin, when it is full-grown, gives birth to death.[14]

How utterly absurd and offensive, then, to thank God for what He says plainly is not from Him.

What has confused many believers is that those who maintain praise for sin works attest to some startling results as proof. The evidence stacked up can be quite convincing. But God often works mercifully on our behalf in spite of ourselves.

Every experience must be judged by the Word of God—not just the results of our spiritual ventures, but the means. The end results never justify unscriptural means. Even miracles performed in Jesus' name do not necessarily have His endorsement. He warned that unless there is explicit obedience to His words, the final act will be personal rejection and divine judgment.[15]

Satan is a slick operator. Why wouldn't he readily let us win a few matches in order to set us up for a smashing defeat? If Satan can induce us to praise for sin because of the "proofs" that it works, he's not beyond baiting us with a multitude of "proofs."

Our Motivation for Praise

When we are scared and hurting, we quickly grab at any teaching that promises a miracle of relief or restoration. This twisted teaching all but guarantees miracles; just start thanking God for whatever the evil, whatever the problem, and it will vanish. Praise God for the sinner's sins, and pronto he'll become a saint.

But this leads me to wonder. If one praised for the single purpose of pleasing God, and not to get answers, would it ever occur to a person to praise Him for sin? And when we praise Him for sin, in all honesty, aren't we playing a manipulation game?

The attempt to manipulate God is no new thing. Praise was a tactic of the Israelites whenever their rebellion got them into trouble. The psalmist tells us about it. "Whenever God slew them, they would seek him; they eagerly turned to him again. . . . But then they would flatter him with their mouths, lying to him with their tongues; their hearts were not loyal to him. . . ."[16]

The truth is that many of us are guilty on this same count. The only reason we are praising God is that we want something from Him. This hypocrisy betrays our love-relationship with God.

Acceptable Praise

The other day I was leafing through my Bible checking out some passages on praise. Suddenly, three words I'd never noticed before stood out as if they were the only words on the page: "Offer right sacrifices."[17]

The word "right" grabbed my attention. How do "right sacrifices" relate to the "sacrifice of praise" which the Bible says we are to offer to God continually?

Since atonement for sin was the first great essential, the sin offering occupied first place. Next, through the burnt offering, the offender dedicated himself to God and His service. Then the grain and peace offerings expressed thankfulness and fellowship with God and the consciousness of being at peace with God.

The laws regarding these offerings were strictly defined. Sacrifices were neither to be offered haphazardly nor according to an individual's whim. "When you sacrifice an offering of thanksgiving to the Lord," God said, "sacrifice it in such a way that it will be accepted on your behalf."[18]

The thank offering was not offered for sin. The only *right* sacrifice for sin was the sin offering. Defilement must first be removed before the thank offering could be acceptable to God.

The relative implications are obvious. Of course temple sacrifices are no longer necessary. Christ once and for all became our sin offering at Calvary. Now we are cleansed from our sin through faith in Christ's shed blood. Now it is the sin offering of Christ that takes first priority in our relationship to God. And now, as then, God's holiness requires that we be cleansed from sin's defilement *before* we offer sacrifices of praise. Only then does praise become a right and acceptable offering.

So what is the touchstone of our faith when dealing with our own sin or in praying for others? It has to be the atonement. And that is something for which it is always legitimate to praise God!

We Praise God for Who He Is

God has given us a remarkable handbook on praise. Born out of the experience of suffering affliction, adversity, and enmity, it is thoroughly practical. When I checked out a hunch, I found the words "tears" and "trouble" and the cry, "Deliver me!" occur more often in the Psalms than in any other book of the Bible. But then, so does the word "praise."

I did not find, however, the psalmist praising God for sin, thanking him for evil. Nothing of the kind! Evil was passionately denounced. The word is, "Let those who love the Lord hate evil."[19]

We find the psalmist praising God for who He is: Creator, Savior, Redeemer, Sustainer of the universe. He extols God's glory, His holiness, His goodness, His majesty, His power, His greatness, His faithfulness, His justice, His righteousness, His abundant grace, His acts of mercy and steadfast love. In the dark hours of personal travail, he praises the God who daily bears us up, who delivered in the past and is yet able to deliver His own.

It is the devil's trick to get us to praise God for the devil's doings rather than to praise for the transcendency of our God. When we are distressed, we cannot praise God as the Source of the problem, but we can always—and should always—praise Him for WHO HE IS.

How to Avoid the Distortions of Praise

Most of us fall far short of the level of praise we find in the Psalms. But we will never rise to their heights if we fall for Satan's distortions of this dynamic principle. It is imperative that we be able to recognize these distortions and to understand the praise that is right and acceptable to God.

This means that I will not join sides with the devil in calling sin good—not in another, lest I open myself to the same sin; not in myself, because I can never cleanse myself by praising God for sin. I can only know cleansing and deliverance through faith in the atonement of Christ. The first step is confession, calling sin what God calls it. But I will praise and thank God for the triumphs of the Cross, for in so doing, I release my faith.

This also means that I must ask God to let me see sin as He sees it, so there won't be any shades of gray in my thinking—or my praising. I will remember how God strictly charged the Old Testament priests to teach God's people, by word and example, how to distinguish between the unclean and the clean. And how God says every believer is a royal priest, chosen to declare His praises. As a believer-priest, I must be every bit as scrupulous in communicating clear-cut distinctions between good and evil. I will not praise God for sin, and thus muddle moral issues. God says He will not tolerate such profaning of His holiness.

I shall stay alert to the possibility that I could be praising God to manipulate Him into giving me what I want. I will remember that praise is never a substitute for obedience.

When I look at a broken, sinful world, I will remember the promise, "He that goeth forth and weepeth, bearing precious seed, shall doubtless come again with rejoicing, bringing his sheaves with him."[20] I pray, therefore, that God will give me tears for the sinner I am trying to bring to Him.

If I find myself under the fire of adversity and trouble, I shall turn to the Psalms and praise directly from God's handbook. I will not focus on the Enemy, but on God! Thus will I praise:

I have seen you in the sanctuary
    and beheld your power and your glory.
Because your love is better than life,
    my lips will glorify you.
I will praise you as long as I live. . . .

Because you are my help,
    I sing in the shadow of your wings.[21]

Deliver me from my enemies, O God;
    protect me from those who rise up against me. . . .

But I will sing of your strength,
    in the morning I will sing of your love;
for you are my fortress,
    my refuge in times of trouble.

O my Strength, I sing praise to you;

> you, O God, are my fortress,
> my loving God.[22]

I shall never brush aside the fact that my commitment to praise must be coupled with a commitment to uprightness of life. Says the psalmist, "It is fitting for the upright to praise him."[23] So as I walk through the day in faith and obedience, "I will praise . . . with an upright heart,"[24] my Lord and my God.

3

Miracles, Anyone?

Although I cannot reach back in memory to that long-ago Sunday morning, I was there when the miracle happened. Mother and Dad were there and never got over the awesome working of God. Again and again I had heard them tell how our friend George had been healed. So I grew up acquainted with a God who healed in the here and now—sovereignly, instantly, unpredictably. For me to deny the miracle would be to deny my own existence.

Out of that experience, I also came to know that miracles in themselves do not produce obedience nor unfaltering commitment to Christ. We are inclined to think that if we were to experience a miracle as George did, we would forever stay on course. Perhaps we would be turned into spiritual giants. But would we?

The Healing of George Hunger

Had you not known that all logging crew foremen are so dubbed, you would have thought "bull o' the woods" was a nickname coined expressly to describe George Hunger. Swarthy, black-haired, a thickset bull moose of a man with powerful shoulders and arms, he had a physique and temperament typical of his Armenian heritage. Every lumberjack in the camp was aware of the Boss's volatile temper. It was scarcely less a threat than the skidding line if a block and cable let loose. When that happened, anyone could be the victim. Even the Boss.

One dreadful day the block and cable cut loose without warning, and it was George who got caught in the bite of the cable. Striking him at the knee, flipping him to the ground, the heavy steel line tore loose the kneecap, leaving his mangled leg contorted, sticking out at a right angle to his thigh.

After being transported a long distance, George was operated on by the most highly skilled surgeons to be found in that area of the Pacific Northwest. In the late 1920s, however, sulfas and antibiotics were not available to fight infection. Even with the most skillful surgery, there was one overshadowing question: "Will it heal?"

Far more likely, gangrene would set in, making amputation imperative. Nevertheless, the doctors decided to operate, encase the leg in a cast from hip to toe, then wait and see.

News of the accident had prompted my mother to pray fervently for George — not for healing, but that his life would be unshackled. Days later she sensed God directing her to visit George and press upon him his need of personal salvation. He listened but made no decision. A couple of days after Mother's visit, a minister stopped in to see George. Before he left, George had committed his life to Christ and knew the reality of being born into God's kingdom. In one divine moment, his life was unshackled—beautifully.

The next Sunday, Dad was guest speaker at the Nazarene church across town. When Mother invited the Hungers to go with us, George objected, saying it would be too much of an ordeal getting him in and out of the car. But Mother saw that as a challenge and said we would stop by to pick them up Sunday morning.

Mother hoped getting George out to church would lift his spirits. He was to report back to the clinic on Monday, and the doctors would then decide whether or not to amputate. He had little hope, fearing the leg was already becoming gangrenous. And even if they could save the leg, he had been warned that the joint fluid had been lost so the knee would always be ramrod stiff.

Following the service that morning, some gathered around the altar to pray. George hobbled down to the front on his crutches to sit in the first pew, his heavy cast stretched out in front of him. He needed to talk to God. The thought of losing his leg was heavy upon him.

Although he had been raised a Roman Catholic, until this past week he had never personally encountered Jesus Christ. Previously, whenever his wife had tried to share with him what it means to be a born-again believer, he had become mean and physically abusive. Now he knew for himself the reality of the new birth, the forgiveness of sins, the assurance of acceptance by God. But there were many perplexities to his newfound faith in the person of Jesus Christ. How could people understand his depression or his confusion?

As far as is known, no one had prayed for George's healing. Who had that kind of faith! If nobody thought to ask the Lord about physical healing, neither did certain of the saints bother to ask God for direction now. George no sooner settled himself in the front pew than God's-little-helpers moved in, huddling around the distraught man, one saying he needed to be "sanctified wholly," another advocating "the baptism with fire."

Later George was to tell how in the midst of his confusion, a silent cry went up from his heart: "O God, give me something by which I can never doubt You again." Then he pulled himself up on his crutches and started for the back of the church.

Halfway up the aisle, Dad stood talking with two or three people. When George reached that point, he reached out his hand to Dad's shoulder. "It was like being hit by three successive bolts of lightning," Dad recounted afterward.

In the same moment, one crutch flew one way, the other clattered in another direction, and George was running down the aisle shouting, "I'm healed! I'm healed!"

At home, George got a knife and went to work removing the cast. Inside, the detached skin lay with the stitches still intact. His leg, now perfectly whole, was without a mark! Every trace of injury—including the surgeon's incision—had disappeared.

At the clinic the next morning, when George walked in without crutches or cast, the nurses rushed to try to force him into a chair. When he pushed them aside and began to dance a rollicking hoedown, they nearly went into hysterics. He was hurried into the examining room, told to pull off his pants, and "helped" onto the table. When asked who had told him to take off the cast, he was radiant: "My Physician did."

After a ring of bewildered doctors had thoroughly examined George, they called in the chief-of-staff. When they showed him the former X-rays, he swore they had the wrong man. "This leg has never been broken!" Finally, convinced that this *was* the same man, the old doctor shook his head. "Sir, I have practiced with Mayo Brothers and the best. I don't know your physician, but I must say, I have never before seen a piece of surgery like this!"

But now the doctors were in another dilemma. What could they do about the insurance forms they had filled out saying this man would be disabled for life?

When George went back to the woods, the men who worked under him did not know what to think about what had happened. But one thing certain, when anything went wrong now, and George met the emergency by sweeping off his hat and dropping to his knees, every hat came off and every man stood at attention until George had finished praying!

Often George would come into Dad's auto repair shop during the week. If, as so often happened, a group of men were standing around the old iron stove talking, George would roll up his pant leg, tell them what God had done, and show them the leg made whole. Tears would soon be coursing down the cheeks of those who listened and saw.

When I was at home for a visit a few years ago, I asked about George Hunger. I knew he must be around eighty years old. Dad's face lit up. He had seen him just a few weeks before on the street downtown. "He's all crippled up with arthritis," Dad told me. "But George said, 'You know, Marsh, I'm in so much pain all the time—everything hurts—except for that leg the Lord healed over forty years ago! I don't have a pain in it!' "

But what about those forty years in between? What might we expect from one who had experienced such a miracle?

A year or so after his miracle, when the church was caught up in all sorts of problems, not the least financial, George was asked to pay his tithe *in advance*. Sure enough, it was just as he had thought!—the church only wanted his paycheck. Bitterly he turned from the church and from God.

Many months later, the Lord used Dad to bring George back to Himself. Rejoicing in the Lord once more, he seemed to go along quite well spiritually. After some time, though, he had again turned back.

The years slipped by, and then our town was stunned by a fiery explosion in the sulphur silo at the pulp mill. Of several men inside at the time, there was only one survivor—George.

How had George been spared when the others had perished? Trapped in an inferno of burning sulphur, George had cried out, "Lord, if You will get me out of here, I will serve You." There was no way out—but George was found on the *outside* of the silo, burned, but not as badly as would be expected. It was another miracle. And now, though his head was "swollen the size of the steering wheel on a new car," he was praising the Lord from his hospital bed, the glory of the Lord's presence filling the room.

I do not know how closely he walked with the Lord after that, but I do know from offhand remarks he made to Dad whenever they happened to meet, that there were long periods of doubt, of floundering, of darkness and discouragement. Whatever the reason, in view of the miracles he had experienced, I found his spiritual reverses difficult to understand.

We have to face it. No matter how much we would like to believe otherwise, miracles of healing do not necessarily produce changed lives. The record of Jesus' healing ministry in the Scriptures makes it very clear that faith is not an inevitable sequence. Neither is gratitude. Some did not even bother to turn and thank the Lord.

Nor, for that matter, do miracles necessarily make believers of the grandstand. The signs and wonders performed by Jesus did attract the astonished people to hear, but they angered those who could not fit the miracles into their structured religion.

Today we still have the thankless, the thrill seekers, the skeptics, the scornful. Others face the miraculous and *do* believe.

The healing of George Hunger forever settled in my mind the reality of supernatural healing. I would never be cheated by someone's puny, limited concept of God. Yet I would discover that some of my responses to the miracle hindered my spiritual growth far into my adult years. To some extent, my own personal healing when I was in a coma near death had the same effect.

But how can the miracles which God so graciously gives to bless us become a stumbling block? The danger lies in our failure to recognize the simple truth that we are all still very much human. This means we need to be aware of the patterns of response that are common to the human psyche. Let me explain.

In our interpersonal relationships, we all use a variety of defense mechanisms, unconscious methods (or from a behavioral point of view, "learned behavior") by which we attempt to protect ourselves from the tension which arises over the conflict between *what we wish we were* and *what we really are*. That we develop defense mechanisms is not all bad. But used inappropriately, they distort reality, and the whole personality tends to become warped.

One ego defense frequently misused by Christians is known as *identification*. Psychologists define this as "the unconscious act of attributing to oneself certain characteristics or traits that one perceives in someone else."[1]

Both *developmental* and *defensive* identification are derived from a desire to be more like another person. This desire is expressed by unconsciously repressing or consciously rejecting the reality of what I am in favor of a self-concept of what I want to be. This pseudo-self-concept is modeled after someone we highly esteem.

Certainly there are useful and positive aspects of identification. Developmental identification plays an important role in child development. For the Christian, identification also plays an important role in counseling and in the ministry of intercession. Identification as a defense mechanism, however, is an impediment for the Christian striving toward spiritual maturity.

Illegitimate identification is a particular hazard for those who move in circles where extraordinary things are happening, where God is confirming His Word and manifesting His power by signs and miracles. It is not at all uncommon for us to associate with men and women of towering spiritual stature and then attribute to ourselves the spiritual qualities we admire in them. Or we identify with the person who has experienced a miracle as if it had happened to us.

Such identification makes an honest assessment of ourselves an impossibility. As long as we court a vicarious sense of spiritual attainment, we will not admit that we are barren and unfruitful. Furthermore, until the Holy Spirit reveals our real motives and attitudes, we will not know our hypocrisy. The Spirit reveals these things only when we are willing to face the pain of change. Until such time, spiritual growth is retarded and spiritual wholeness thwarted.

How do I know? It happened to me. Because I knew George and was there when it happened—and because my parents had been involved in his healing—I had unconsciously clung to some personal spiritual advantage until I began to entreat God to deal with every bit of phoniness in my life.

The Holy Spirit brought to my conscious level the identification I had appropriated from this miracle. It showed up under His spotlight as simulated spirituality. There was no denying the miserable implications. For me to assume any measure of spiritual attainment because of my presence or my parents' involvement was stupid to say the least. Even worse, I had been seeking some sort of illegitimate recognition—spiritual status seeking, no less. Pride, condescension, self-deception—all were involved. And I knew God hated these things.

What then?

Whatever the plague of the heart, the remedy is the same. Confession, repentance, forgiveness, cleansing, a change of direction. But once the past is set in order, how are we to regard and respond to the miraculous?

To prevent a recurrence of negative effects, we need to take a closer look at the causes within ourselves. Here we need the Holy Spirit's help, and absolute honesty.

In varying degrees, our behavior-coping strategies stem from feelings of inadequacy and lack of self-worth. Our ego defenses become exaggerated to the degree that we feel we need to compensate for our defects and deficiencies. But trying to compensate by seeing ourselves as possessing the faith, virtues, spiritual gifts, or ministry of another, is self-deception. And the self-deception which seizes upon spurious spirituality will seek to impress others at every opportunity.

Do you recall certain Corinthian Christians exhibiting this sort of behavior? Could anything be more absurd than these saints quarreling among themselves over who was the most spiritual? Ranking themselves according to whose disciple they were, they clamored for recognition on the basis, "I belong to Paul," or "I belong to Apollos," or "I belong to Cephas," or "I belong to Christ."[2] No doubt each one also paraded the number of converts he had made and the miracles he had witnessed as further proof of spiritual superiority.

Paul speaks bluntly to the situation. "Let no one deceive himself. . . . For it is written, 'He catches the wise in their craftiness,' and again, 'The Lord knows that the thoughts of the wise are futile.' So let no one boast of men."[3]

Paul's recognition of this common tendency prompted a similar warning to the Romans. "Do not think of yourself more highly than you ought, but rather think of yourself with sober judgment, in accordance with the measure of faith God has given you."[4]

He goes on to instruct believers to function in each particular situation specifically as God has ordained each one's personal gift of faith should operate. If we heed Paul's injunction, we won't need to wave the flag of another man's faith, nor will we have a pseudo testimony because of our inappropriate identification.

Presuming Upon God and Our Past

The reality of spiritual life in the here-and-now does not allow me to claim status by my own past spiritual experiences either. To have witnessed the divine, to have experienced the miraculous power of God in my life in the past, does not prove anything about where I am in God this moment.

Although my own life was miraculously restored from near death, I have come to understand that the spiritual experiences and miracles of yesterday are just that. Moreover, miracles should always be viewed as evidences of God's grace. They say nothing about my righteousness or any special favor with God.

This is clearly evidenced by Israel's history. During the

Israelites' forty-year trek to Canaan, miracles were the daily experience of every man, woman, and child.

But did this mean that they all knew the same obedience of faith and intimate communion with Jehovah? Hardly! Of the vast multitude who came out of Egypt, only Caleb and Joshua remained steadfast in faith, "wholly following the Lord." The rest discovered to their sorrow that to have experienced a miracle wasn't the sort of credential God was looking for. The miracles which had been an expression of God's love and mercy were neither earned nor effected by any man. Miracles did not prove squatters' rights in Canaan!

What they did not see, and what we must recognize, is the moral obligation which miracles do incur. We cannot escape the personal responsibility brought by the touch of God upon our life, the revelation of His ways.

In recounting the miraculous provision Israel had known as God's chosen, the prophets relentlessly spoke of Israel's failure to respond appropriately. Like spoiled, irresponsible children, they complained about almost everything. The depth of their ingratitude was evident in their turning to follow heathen gods.

Incredible! Time after time, they turned the very miracle of divine provision into a fetish or idol or center of cultish worship.

In one such case God had graciously provided the "brazen serpent" which Moses raised up on a pole in the midst of the camp. Here was Israel's touchstone of healing, a symbol of Christ who would be raised up on a cross to bring eternal life to sin-sick humanity. The sick had only to "look at it and live."[5]

But the day came when King Hezekiah smashed the bronze serpent to bits. Why? Because the people now called it *Nehushtan* and burned incense to it. Though they had been strictly forbidden to worship or bow their knee to any image made with hands, they were doing it. The object itself had become a god to them.[6]

And look at what happened at Bethel in the very place where Jacob had seen a vision and God had promised, "a nation and a company of nations shall come from you, and kings shall spring from you." Here where God had named Jacob "the father of Israel," and Jacob had named the spot "the throne of God,"

Jeroboam set up a golden calf and the people worshiped before it.[7]

In Gilgal also, where the Israelites first camped after crossing the Jordan, and where the Passover was first eaten in the Promised Land, worship degenerated into sordid and licentious practices. Israel not only misused her blessings, but again and again those places and objects associated with the miraculous manifestation of the divine presence became the sites of flagrant disobedience. Those upon whom God had lavished His love became an anguish and abomination to Him.

And then there were those who expected God to accommodate His miracles to their selfishness. Remember how the Israelites were instructed to gather only enough manna each morning for that day? But some gathered enough for two days, so they could sleep late the next morning. When they reached for their breakfast on that second morning, they found the leftover manna crawling with worms.

On the other hand, though the people had been instructed to gather twice the usual amount of manna in preparation for the Sabbath, those who did not bother went out on the seventh day and found none.[8] And who did they blame? God!—just as they blamed Him for everything else.

As outlandish as such conduct seems, I doubt if those folks acted so differently from some of us. The point is that God is not obligated to perform according to our whims, nor have we any right to presume upon His favor or His mercy.

Growth Is Essential

Identifying the dangers in being exposed to the miraculous should cause us to appreciate more fully Peter's admonition to "add to your faith. . . ." Significantly, Peter directed his words to "those who through the righteousness of our God and Savior Jesus Christ have received a faith as precious as ours."[9] Not through their own righteousness, but only through the righteousness of God did they, or we, obtain this faith.

But is this enough? Peter foresaw the future and knew he did not have much longer to live. He foresaw false teachers moving in to deceive many. He declared that the resources of God—"everything we need for life and godliness"—are available to prevent spiritual dearth or disaster because of deception.

"For this very reason," he urges, "make every effort to add to your faith, goodness; and to goodness, knowledge; and to knowledge, self-control; and to self-control, perseverance; and to perseverence, godliness; and to godliness, brotherly kindness; and to brotherly kindness, love."[10]

In other words, Peter is saying, "If you don't want to end up a spiritual casualty, *don't stagnate spiritually!*"

The Blessings and the Dangers

I have come a long way, both in time and distance, from the scene of George Hunger's remarkable healing. But the impact has not diminished: God heals in the here-and-now—sovereignly, instantly, unpredictably.

I have also come a long way in understanding the dangers that accompany any visible display of divine power. I have seen the need to guard against illegitimate identification, and I am aware of the importance of exercising discernment whenever I am faced by the supernatural. Also, I have come to realize that every encounter with the miraculous must be integrated into the whole counsel of God. Otherwise, these experiences can prove more detrimental than beneficial to our spiritual growth and maturity.

Never does our bungling of God's blessings negate the authenticity of a divine miracle nor indicate fault on God's part. Without exception, the problem lies with us, and part of it may be our need to accept ourselves. It is important that we understand: *It is all right to be me—even if I haven't walked on water*.

If, on the other hand, the Lord says, "Come," and walking on water is a matter of obedience, that is another thing. We must always obey His commands. But we don't have to fake anything. Ever.

By allowing the Holy Spirit to surface and deal with any illegitimate identification, we can begin to minister out of what God has invested in us. Our identification will be with Christ, and it will be for real.

In giving us the Holy Spirit, Christ has made available tremendous power—but not for playing games. *We are never to manipulate or exploit divine power.* We are to be channels through which the power of the Holy Spirit flows at God's bidding.

Therefore, I constantly pray, **for myself** and for others, that the Holy Spirit will teach us how to **receive** the gifts of spiritual, mental, emotional, and physical healing. Faith to receive according to the Father's will—yes! But to become enamored with the spectacular—never!

Finally, I would have to say that while I am different today because of the miracles I have experienced, my relationship with God can be experienced only in the present moment. My commitment to the lordship of Christ can be attested to only by my immediate "Yes, Lord," in response to His voice. *Nothing,* not even the most profound miracle, will ever be as important to my spiritual growth as my quick and ready obedience.

I am still thrilled by every visible manifestation of the power of the risen Christ, and I am deeply grateful for the healings in our family and in others. But I have learned the importance of keeping miracles in their proper perspective. This means checking up on myself often: Am I in any way claiming some spiritual advantage for having been used as a channel of God's healing or deliverance power? Do I ever become so excited by the supernatural signs and wonders that I miss His voice?

Or can I honestly say that Christ himself is the center of my attention?

4

It's the Real Thing—Or Is It?

Slain in the Spirit
Speaking in Tongues
Perfect Peace

The Lord has given us fair warning: "My thoughts are not your thoughts, neither are your ways my ways" (Isa. 55:8). Still, many of us question any unconventional move of God. People being slain in the Spirit, speaking in tongues and experiencing "perfect peace" create tensions by upsetting religious traditions. Too, we are afraid of what we do not understand.

No matter, God still moves sovereignly for our good and His glory. And those of us who are open to the various ways God chooses to manifest himself make a joyous discovery: His ways truly are higher than our ways.

God also has warned us that Satan skillfully counterfeits His ways and His good gifts. We are not to accept blindly all mystical experience as genuine. We must learn to distinguish between what is of Satan and what is of God. Let's look at some of the ways we can tell the difference.

Slain in the Spirit

It was my second summer at our denomination's girls' camp. Betty was the sparkly blue-eyed brunette who bunked across from me. During the day, we romped through the various camp activities; every evening we gathered in the rustic chapel for vespers. After a hearty sing-time, a missionary from India spoke to us. Following the talk, an invitation was given for those who wanted to commit their lives to Christ.

On Wednesday night the girls who responded lined the smooth plank bench which served as an altar. Betty knelt among them. Moments later she was stretched out on the floor, apparently unconscious. The camp director, a pastor's wife, was beside her in an instant. She tenderly lifted the slim sixteen-year-old in her arms and laid her on the altar. "Betty's perfectly all right," she assured the frightened faces in the room. "The Lord is talking to her. When He finishes, she will be fine."

Though it was not the first time I had seen someone "fall under the power," most of the campers had no idea what was happening. For the moment, attention was diverted from Jackie who was seated on a bench against the wall. In trouble with the law, Jackie was a girl whose church had sponsored her week at camp in hopes she would come to know Christ. Campers and staff had been intensely praying for her. At the conclusion of the message, two girls had gone to Jackie and tried to persuade her to give herself to Jesus. Her jaw set, she eyed them disdainfully. But now, all eyes were on the motionless girl on the altar.

Suddenly, Betty sat up, her arms raised straight over her head. In one swift movement, she swung her legs off the bench, shot over to where Jackie was sitting, and dropped to her knees in front of the girl. "Oh, Jackie!" she cried, "I've just been to heaven. It was so beautiful. . . ." Pouring out a glowing account of what she had just seen, Betty begged Jackie to accept Jesus as her Savior—she mustn't miss heaven!

Breaking into tears, Jackie knelt down and began to cry out for the Lord to save her. The Lord had sovereignly moved in our midst.

Another such sovereign move of God's hand was witnessed by my father.

When Dad was a young preacher, he occasionally paired up with one of the old-time evangelists to conduct tent meetings. Some communities where they set up tent were skeptical, others were outright antagonistic.

In one town, one of the leaders of the opposition was the local doctor's wife. At the close of the evening service, a young woman had come forward asking for prayer that God would heal her. Emaciated from TB, she was obviously very sick. As she knelt at the altar with her friends around her, she tried to hold up her hands to pray. Too weak to do so, she asked the girls to hold them up for her.

The doctor's wife, who had been standing at the back of the tent, was furious. Anyone could see that the girl was dying; holding up her hands was cruel. She determined to put a stop to such foolishness. Down the aisle she stormed, kicking sawdust as she went, rolling up her sleeves to do battle. Halfway to the front, she dropped as if she'd been shot. The power of God had struck her. Someone threw a coat over her, and when she came to some minutes later, she got up and sneaked out the back without uttering a sound. Needless to say, there was no more harassment in that place.

Years later in his travels, Dad spoke at a church where a woman came up to him and said, "I'm sure you don't remember me. When I was a girl, dying with TB, you prayed for me. . . ." She had been completely healed, was married, and had a family. When the doctor's wife set out to interrupt the work of the Great Physician, God had dramatically intervened.

I suspect that some who read this will not understand the term "slain in the Spirit." And many of those who do, think it is unique to the charismatic renewal or a Kathyrn Kuhlman meeting. But this phenomenon is not something new; it shows up again and again in church history. Other terms are also used to express that the Spirit of the Lord came upon someone: "falling under the power," "falling backward," "trances," "strikings," "prostrations," "transport," "rapture," "ravishment," or "ecstasies."

The *Encyclopedic Dictionary of Religion* describes the phenomenon this way:

> Ecstasy (in the Bible), a word of Greek origin meaning displacement. Biblically, it refers to a psychic displacement by which someone is so controlled by the Spirit of God that his men-

tal facilities and some normal functions are held wholly or partly in suspension because of an intense emotional or mystical experience that absorbs all consciousness. . . . Ecstasy arises, not from mere emotional rapture, but from the Spirit of Yahweh which falls upon a person, takes control of the center of the self, and makes him an instrument of divine will.[1]

As for biblical examples, we know Ezekiel received many of his prophecies while he was in an ecstatic trance. Moreover, the Apostle John, writing the Revelation, said, "On the Lord's Day I was in the Spirit." Given a dazzling vision of Christ, he recorded this reaction: "When I saw him, I fell at his feet as though dead."[2]

Likewise, the priests in the Old Testament "could not stand to minister by reason of the cloud: for the glory of the Lord had filled the house of God."[3]

In the Bible, many of those flattened by the power of God were unbelievers. The soldiers who came to arrest Jesus in the garden fell backward to the ground. Saul of Tarsus, bent on wiping out the Christian Church, was struck down in the dust of the Damascus road.

Throughout the centuries, mystics frequently mentioned falling into a state of ecstasy. Saint Teresa (1515-1582), who William James said "is the expert of experts in describing such conditions," wrote:

In the orison [prayer] of union, the soul is fully awake as regards God, but wholly asleep as regards things of this world and in respect of herself. . . . In short, she is utterly dead to the things of the world and lives solely in God. . . . I do not even know whether in this state she has enough life to breathe. It seems to me she has not; or at least that if she does breathe, she is unaware of it. . . . So a person who falls into a deep faint appears as if dead. . . .

Thus does God, when he raises a soul to union with himself, suspend the natural action of all her faculties. She neither sees, hears, nor understands, so long as she is united with God. But this time is always short, and it seems even shorter than it is. God establishes himself in the interior of this soul in such a way, that when she returns to herself, it is wholly impossible for her to doubt that she has been in God, and God in her.[4]

Ecstasies came to be regarded by directors of Roman Catholic piety "as an act of grace accorded by God as an encouragement to beginners." Aspirants after holiness were instructed "not to be disquieted by the cessation of such favors since this is the normal course of education in the inward life."[5]

Accounts of the well-known Protestant revivals during the 1700s, 1800s, and early 1900s note that mystical states often occurred. During the Welsh revivals, one reporter wrote, "It is not a question of one town being awakened, but of the whole principality being on fire." Trances, he stated, were common.[6]

McKay (1890), writing of revival, said:

> It is well known that in Ireland, infidels and scoffers who came to see and ridicule the work were frequently stricken down, and thus convicted and converted and made monuments to the power of the Spirit of God. So it was the great awakening of 1859 was known as *Annus Mirabilis*—a year of wonders—in Ulster.[7]

Wherever outpourings of the Spirit swept through England, Scotland, Wales, Ireland, Canada or the United States in a general awakening, ecstasies and the like were reported among Presbyterians, Congregationalists, Baptists, and Methodists alike— long before there were Pentecostal denominations.

In fact, the Free Methodist camp meetings I attended as a child were zealously anti-Pentecostal. Yet I saw men and women slain in the Spirit on numerous occasions. There was one marked difference, however, between those incidents and much of what happens today. No one caught anyone! It was an unspoken rule—you didn't touch what God was doing. Catching wasn't necessary; no one got hurt falling.

Certainly any genuine manifestation of God's presence is awesome. But it is downright scary to watch someone try to manipulate God, a congregation, or individuals, in order to "prove" God's presence and power. And since the attraction for the ecstatic is as old as life itself, Satan has no trouble finding men and women willing to cooperate.

I sat on the platform at a large conference and watched as the speaker urged people to come forward for deliverance from cigarettes by prayer and laying on of hands. There was nothing wrong with that, but what happened next left me shaken and angry.

First, it was explained that when hands were laid on those

standing, they would likely fall backward. So, strong men were lined up to catch them. When everyone was properly positioned, the ones wanting deliverance were told to put their hands up and start praising God. The speaker moved rapidly down the line. A hand to the forehead, a quick forceful shove, and one after another toppled like dominoes—not because they fell against each other, but because the psychological effect produced a similar reaction.

Quite like a game we played as children: hold out your arms, close your eyes, and try to stay on your feet when the person who is "it" gives you a sudden quick shove. But it was only a child's game—if we went sprawling backward, we didn't pretend God did it.

Here, however, the power of suggestion was employed along with physical force. Expected to fall, and pushed off balance, people fell. But this was not children at play; this was a charismatic conference. And the crowd was told that they were witnessing the power of God—that these men and women were being "slain in the Spirit." It was gross deception.

One further word of caution here. Don't think just because a person is not pushed, it is necessarily God causing him to fall. Psychological forces alone can cause people to fall backward. Even without consciously imitating the experience of others, it is easy for someone to fall when he craves mystical experiences. Much falling down may well be self-induced.

There is always the possibility that the person has genuinely been touched by God—in spite of the exploiters. But if what occurs is merely a physical or psychological response, the danger is that of believing that one has experienced divine reality. Later, such deception often gives rise to acute spiritual confusion.

As for those who practice this sort of deception, if they are not already deceived themselves, they certainly open themselves to the worst sort of delusion. The Bible makes this plain and warns of certain judgment for those who dare to exploit any divine manifestation or try to play God.

Most of us want to know how we can be certain what is real. And we want to know how to understand the genuine.

Frankly, it is not always easy to sort out the real from the fake. Think back to the account of Moses confronting Pharaoh with the reality of Almighty Jehovah by casting his rod to the ground where it immediately became a slithering serpent. But then, not only did the king's wizards duplicate this miracle, but they were also able to turn water into blood and cause frogs to appear from seemingly nowhere.[8]

Here we have stark evidence that supernatural acts prove nothing about a person's relationship to God, or that God is necessarily the source of the power. If there is any question about the experience, maintain the attitude: wait and see. If we stay around a little longer, we may find, as did Pharaoh, that the wizard's serpents are swallowed up by Moses' rod. And in the end, the supernatural powers of the pseudo-miracle workers or the performances of the play actors fail in confrontation with the omnipotent power of the living God.

Still, when it comes to spiritual ecstasies of any kind, there is one significant clue to help us evaluate what is of God and what is not. It is this: the real generally happens *spontaneously*. No one sets the stage. As one commentator points out, "Those [spiritual ecstasies] not propagated by contagion, and which contain a strong moral and intellectual as well as emotional element, are at once the rarest and the most trustworthy."[9]

I share my own experience of these matters with reluctance because I am aware that expectations can be primed. And that I spurn. Yet, to make my point clear, I need to say what I myself have seen.

Never will I forget my surprise and bewilderment the first time someone I prayed for fell, apparently under the power of God. Till then, I assumed the person ministering must feel a force like electricity flowing through him to the one for whom he is praying. But I felt nothing—except God's presence and the assurance that I was acting in obedience. Yet my fingers barely brushed the man when he went down. A SAC Air Force officer, he was hardly the emotional, hysterical type.

The next day, I spoke at a dinner meeting. Afterward, as I prayed for an ex-prostitute, she slumped to the floor without warning. This time, I recognized demonic intrusion. I did the one thing I always do in such a situation: I held up the lordship of Christ. Kneeling beside the woman, I declared Jesus Christ Lord of lords and King of kings; I declared that He defeated Satan and all his imps at Calvary, that He is Victor over every evil force that would destroy this woman, and that Jesus Christ was present and no evil power could stand before Him. Within minutes, the woman was set free.

A man looking on said that he, too, wanted to be free from an enslaving habit. "You can," I said. "You saw what happened to her." I meant being set free—not falling on the floor. But when I started to pray for him, he so obviously tried to duplicate what he had seen that I could have bit my tongue for having unintentionally slipped him that suggestion.

Because of this early experience, along with what I've seen since, I'm quicker to spot the false. And I'm less impressed when people start falling en masse. I expressly avoid putting any premium on any physical manifestation of the Spirit. Above all, I know that if a person is genuinely slain in the Spirit, it is not I but God who has sovereignly touched that person's spirit.

It is a mistake to attribute the power to the one ministering. The evidence indicates that the power does not come from an outside force or dynamic energy emanating from the one ministering. Rather, a person is "slain in the Spirit" when an "illumination from God, affecting the intellect and the will, is of such intensity that the physical powers and external senses are too weak to withstand it."[10] Or put simply, it is the person's physical reaction to the presence of a holy God. This is why, when true mystical experiences do occur, there is often a special anointing of God on the service.

In assessing the authenticity of any mystical experience, we have a right to question any experience described only in terms of physical euphoria and emotional exaltation. I find nothing in the Bible to indicate that God's purpose in any divine visitation is a state of ecstasy. Rather, I find God reveals himself in order to transform lives. Inflated emotions or physical reactions are only incidental. The paramount issue is: How closely and consistently does the person walk with the Lord in the days ahead?

To be sure, we cannot discount an experience simply because

the person does not go on to walk in obedience. At the same time, "when we see error, sin, and selfishness giving way to truth, holiness, and love—we say unhesitatingly, this is not the work of Satan, but a great and glorious work of God.[11]

Christians need always to be careful to differentiate between the incidentals accompanying a visitation of God and what is fundamental—the inner work of the Holy Spirit. Such discrimination would prevent our making too much of mystical experiences as such. It would also do much to prevent the deceptive practices of those who strive to incite the spectacular. What all this comes down to is that we must rivet our attention upon our *commitment* and *obedience* to the Lord Jesus Christ rather than upon the phenomena which may not be occurring around us. Otherwise we can easily be deceived.

Speaking in Tongues

Several years ago I ran into another problem that has plagued the charismatic renewal. After speaking at a ladies' luncheon, I went to counsel a woman who was crying uncontrollably. When I asked if she had a burden she wanted to share, she shook her head. "No, I don't have any problems. . . . I don't know what is wrong."

She insisted she had a good marriage, a good relationship with her son, no health problems, and no financial worries.

"No problems!" I smiled to myself. Maybe we should trade places and she should be doing the counseling.

Still, I knew there had to be a reason for the anguish in her eyes and the wrenching sobs. I asked about her relationship to the Lord. Did she know Christ as her Savior? Had she truly been born from above?

She looked puzzled.

A year ago a prominent preacher had prayed for her and she had spoken in tongues, she said. She wondered if this is what I meant.

The ensuing conversation revealed that she knew nothing about *repentance* and *regeneration*. She had had a "tongues experience"—nothing more. She did not have a sound spiritual foundation at all. Yet the one who had prayed for her likely went merrily on his way boasting of how many people he baptized with the Spirit. The truth is that whatever had happened was not the Holy Spirit's work.

The confusion comes from equating any expression of tongues with the baptism in the Holy Spirit. We need to keep in mind that there is a true Spirit-given gift of tongues. But there are also counterfeit tongues which come from Satan. There may also be simply human tongues—it appears that every person has the built-in capacity to speak in tongues. (Could it be that in some cases the person somehow breaks through into this dimension on his own?)

In any case, a "tongues experience" which is not truly from the Holy Spirit is sure to create problems. I have listened to heartrending accounts of near mental and emotional breakdowns from those who found themselves in this situation. The lady who had been so sure that she had no problems is one example. As I talked further with her, deep-rooted, long-standing fears surfaced. Not only did she need salvation, she would need much prayer, counseling, sound Bible teaching, and the strong support of spiritually mature Christians to be set free and established in Christ.

The flow of the Spirit in the language of the Spirit can be a catharsis bringing inner harmony and wholeness to body, soul, and spirit. If, instead, we find praying in tongues is accompanied by fear and confusion, we need to check out the reason. Whether one prays in English or in a Spirit-given prayer language, it is absolutely crucial to one's mental and emotional health to be wholly committed to the lordship of Christ—to the known and unknown will of God. To pray prayers initiated by the Holy Spirit and according to God's will when one is really bent on pleasing oneself can create shattering inner conflicts.

Perfect Peace

Just as men and women can be deluded into accepting counterfeit religious phenomenon as real, they can be fooled into thinking God is the source of all subjective feelings of love and peace.

In Agatha Christie's autobiography I came across an incident that gave me chills, so superbly did Satan counterfeit the peace of God. Telling of her visit to the shrine of Sheikh Adi in Northern Iraq, Agatha Christie wrote:

> . . . accompanied by a policeman, we walked up a winding path. It was spring, fresh and green, with wild flowers all the way. There was a mountain stream. We passed occasional goats and children. Then we reached the Yezedi shrine. The peacefulness of it comes back—the flagged courtyard, the black snake carved on the wall of the shrine. Then the step carefully *over*, not *on* the threshold, into the small dark sanctuary. There we sat in the courtyard under a gently rustling tree. One of the Yezidees brought us coffee, first carefully spreading a dirty tablecloth. (This, proudly, as showing that European needs were understood.) We sat there a long time. Nobody forced information on us. I knew, vaguely, that the Yezidees were devil worshippers, and the Peacock Angel, Lucifer, is the object of their worship. It always seems strange that the worshippers of Satan should be the most peaceful of all the varying religious sects in that part of the world. When the sun began to get low, we left. It had been utter peace.[12]

As I read this, I thought how tragic that anyone would consciously allow her spirit to blend in utter harmony with the spiritual world of devil worship. To do so would surely open oneself to the evil spirits of Satan's domain.

Aside from that, the above scene raises a disturbing question: Can Christians be fooled into thinking Satan's counterfeit is the peace of God?

They certainly can. We see the evidence when someone does what the Bible plainly condemns, yet maintains it must be okay because they have perfect peace doing it. Obviously the person is deceived, for according to the Bible, obedience is absolutely essential if one is to know the peace of God.

Attempting to prepare the disciples for His departure, Jesus assured them that the Holy Spirit would comfort, counsel, teach, and guide them. Then He added, "Peace I leave with you; my peace I give you. I do not give to you as the world gives. Do not let your hearts be troubled and do not be afraid."[13]

Here, as He frequently did, Jesus pointed out the antithesis between His way and the way of the world. Does He say the world does not give peace? No, but He says there is a difference. The world sees peace as the absence of trouble; eliminate stress and strain, pressure and conflict, and one will know peace. On the contrary, Jesus taught that the peace He gives does not depend on circumstances, but is based on our relationship with God.

Paul underscored this same truth: "Since we have been justified through faith, we have peace with God through our Lord Jesus Christ."[14] Clearly, peace is not a mere feeling, but a fact.

Of course it's possible for one who is not a Christian to enjoy a sense of serenity in the midst of a tranquil backdrop. But if you and I are rightly related to God, we can quietly trust in His purposes even when the whole world is in upheaval.

Paul, though lashed by the gales of adversity, was a shining example of a man whose thoughts were guarded by "the peace of God, which transcends all understanding."[15] The Spirit of Jesus, having taken possession of his heart, mind, and will, brought forth the fruit of peace. With his quiet, settled heart, what a marvel Paul must have been to the sailors on board the Rome-bound ship caught in the fury of a northeaster.

When someone paints the Christian life as a restful rose garden secluded from hardship, reverses, and calamity, I think of a favorite quotation of mine. "The man who possessed it [peace] was not exempt from storm or shipwreck, but *by faith he knew he would arrive in port*. . . . And so where all else was panic, he played the man."[16] (Emphasis mine.)

It was the quiet calm of the Moravian brethren during a storm at sea that awakened John Wesley to something missing in his own faith. Even though he was on his way to America as a missionary, he had not experienced redemption and the assurance of salvation which these brethren spoke about. Nor did he know the intimate fellowship with Christ which produced such utter abandonment to God's will that there was no agitation over circumstances.

When Wesley returned to England, he experienced a profound conversion. "I felt I did trust in Christ, Christ alone, for salvation; and an assurance was given me that He had taken away my sins," he reported. He went on to become a fearless preacher, undaunted by the opposition of his own Anglican church. Not surprisingly, a particular emphasis of Wesley's doctrine was the necessity of all believers having an experience of "perfect love which casts out all fear."[17]

You and I must never forget that peace which is not centered in God and in the crucified and risen Christ is nothing more than an illusion. Casting about for peace in any other way—through philosophies, religious movements, mystical experiences—exposes us to deception.

In the fourteenth chapter of John, Jesus reassures His disciples that they will share in His ultimate victory over the world. "I have told you these things," He said, "so that in me you might have peace."[18] Only as we *abide in Christ* can we know true peace.

Peace, Paul tells us, is one fruit of the Spirit. But think of the conditions under which the fruit of the Spirit was produced in Paul's life!—"in great endurance; in troubles, hardships and distresses; in beatings, imprisonments and riots; in hard work, sleepless nights and hunger."[19]

Thus the distinction is clear-cut. The peace that the world gives is a dead end—it ends when the hurricane hits, it goes *poof* in the earthquake and fire. Not so the peace of God. Proper relationships based on *God's forgiveness* and *our obedience* assure inner tranquillity *amidst* trouble. This is the peace which is real.

We may be momentarily stunned by the blows of life. But if we continue to abide in Christ, the Prince of Peace himself will see us through suffering, humiliation, and distress. Not only will He provide spiritual security, but He will enable us to march out of the valley singing lustily: "Thanks be to God, who always leads us in triumphal procession in Christ and through us spreads everywhere the fragrance of the knowledge of him."[20]

5

The Battle of the Sexes— Headship/Submission

I could scarcely believe what I was hearing. . . .

Having arrived on an early morning flight, I was in an eastern city having breakfast with the two women who had met me at the airport. They wanted to know if I agreed with the prominent speaker who told them the truly submissive wife would be a prostitute if her husband told her to do so. This man had suggested that if the wife had enough faith, God might pull off a last-minute rescue operation. But regardless, she was to obey and not talk back.

Incredible as it seemed that Christians would pay attention to such rubbish, many put this principle into practice. Not that husbands pressed their wives to become prostitutes. They simply adopted the grossly distorted idea that the husband was to have autocratic control. Marriages of many couples who have tried to live by these teachings soon founder, both the husband and wife being devastated by the effect.

Mishandling the Truth

This evil was launched in the Garden of Eden. When Satan approached Eve, he was obsessed with one thing—gaining autocratic control. By deceiving the mother of the human race, he would bring all her descendants under his authority and enslave them in eternal bondage. What was his snaky tactic? Distortion—twisting what God said. It was a tactic that proved a masterstroke of deception, and Satan continues to use it with alarming success.

Paul wasn't speaking to a problem peculiar to the Ephesian church when he warned the elders, "Even from your own number men will arise and distort the truth in order to draw away disciples after them."[1] The devil's advocates are still with us—charming, popular, super salespersons. And their twisted teaching is often beamed at illicit control.

No subject has seen more chaotic debate then the subject of authority-submission. And no aspect of authority-submission has engendered more distorted teaching than that of women's role in society, in marriage, and in the Church.

In recent years, the move of the Holy Spirit has created a hunger in men and women not only to know what God's Word says, but how to relate it to every detail of their lives. In their eagerness to learn God's ways, many have gobbled up everything that is peddled from podium and printed page. The trouble is that not everyone mouthing Scripture teaches sound doctrine. False statements often slip by unnoticed under the credence of a popular by-line. Or because of the striking truths presented, the unsuspecting and undiscerning swallow the error along with the truth.

This ambush of Satan—teaching based on misrepresentation of Scripture—works because many Christians never check the accuracy of what they read or hear. They assume that if a highly esteemed minister or revered authority figure claims that the Bible teaches thus and so, it must be true. Here's an example of how wrong this assumption can be.

Writing on the role of women, a well-known Bible teacher quoted 1 Timothy 3:1 (KJV): "This is a true saying, if a man desires the office of a bishop. . . ." After the word "man" he inserted in parentheses "not woman." Here is proof, he said, that women have no place in ministry or leadership roles. But he must have known that the Greek work translated here in the KJV as "man" is a generic term, the indefinite pronoun *tis* meaning "any person."

To further prove his case, he quoted, "If any man speak, let him speak as the oracles of God. . ." (1 Pet. 4:11, KJV). Peter's use of the word "man" as opposed to "woman," he declared, excluded all women from preaching or teaching. The Greek word here is *anthropos*, referring to any member of the human race. Had Peter wished to stress maleness, he would have used the Greek word *aner*.

The writer went on, "Nowhere in the Bible does it say women are to rule." But again, not so! Paul says wives *are to rule* their own households.[2]

What's more, there is a significant difference between this word "rule" and the one Paul uses when advising Timothy that elders are to *rule* their own households well.[3] When he speaks of elders ruling their households, Paul uses the term *proistemi*, which means "stand before." But when he counsels younger widows to marry and *"rule* their households" (RSV), he uses the word *oikodespoteo*, a very strong Greek word meaning "unlimited rule" or "absolute master." (The KJV translates *oikodespoteo* "guide," the NIV "manage.") "Despot," "despotic," and "despotism" are its English derivatives.

We would be in error if we took this statement to mean that a wife has the right to impose her will on her husband. That is not what the Apostle meant. Still, Paul says plainly that young widows should marry, bear children, and exercise absolute or uncontrolled rule over their households. To write that "nowhere in the Bible does it say women are to rule" is to write untruth.

What upset me most about the article was that I knew many would believe every word simply because the by-line was a popular name. But Christians can't afford to be so gullible. No matter who it is that claims, "The Bible says . . . ," we need to carefully check out the truth.

Sarah—Our Example

Many Bible teachers and preachers are more given to imagination than to careful exegesis. And who among them is going to mention those scriptures which would raise questions and support some other view? Tradition and strong prejudice also give rise to distortion and misapplication of truth. I can think of no better example than the story of Sarah and Abraham.

Take Sarah—the woman we've been persuaded was the epitome of submissiveness, the ideal model for all Christian women. Didn't she call Abraham, "Lord"? Wasn't she perfectly obedient? And her lying—was it not a spiritual virtue stemming from total submission to her husband? A truly spiritual woman will follow suit, we are told, because, quoting Peter, "this is the way holy women of the past who put their hope in God used to make themselves beautiful."[4]

There, the quoters stop. Or they breeze over the rest of what Peter says, namely, "You are her daughters if you do what is right and do not give way to fear."[5]

As I studied this passage, it struck me: What was Peter's point? What did he mean by *do what is right and do not give way to fear*"?

Turning back to Genesis, I began to outline carefully the relationship of Abraham and Sarah to each other—and to the Covenant. In no time, I was making notations that totally contradicted all the sermons I'd heard about Abraham and Sarah.

For instance, the storytellers had Sarah painting the nursery and knitting blue booties in anticipation of a promised son twenty-five years before Isaac's birth. But the time element didn't fit the facts. And wasn't her purpose in giving Hagar to Abraham to fulfill God's promise? That's not what the Bible says. Was Sarah the totally submissive wife? Let's trace the events from the beginning.

Abraham was seventy-five years old when God called him out of Ur, promising that through his offspring all nations would be blessed. His line would be perpetuated, his name great and known to all generations. But ten years ticked by, and Abraham and Sarah remained childless. Had God forgotten His promise? Baffled, Abraham confronted God with his disappointment: the way things stood, one of his household servants would be his heir.

"No," God said. "Eliezer is not the promised seed. But a son coming from your own body will be your heir. And you will no more be able to count your descendants than you can count the stars."[6]

We don't know whether or not Abraham talked any of this over with his wife. But the evidence indicates he did not.

In that culture, childlessness was a grief and a reproach. Like any Jewish wife, Sarah wanted a family—one way or another—so in keeping with the practice of that day, Sarah gave her personal maid to Abraham. Perhaps Abraham anticipated that sleeping with Hagar would produce the promised child. But was that Sarah's motive? Not according to her. She said, "The Lord has kept me from having children . . . perhaps I can build a family through her."[7] Unlike Hannah, who looked to God to take away her reproach of barrenness, Sarah had her own plan, and Abraham went along with it, not bothering to check with God. So the child Ishmael was born to Hagar when Abraham was eighty-six. Not the child of the Promise, but a child of their own fleshly desires.

Thirteen years later, Abraham again hears from the Lord about the matter of the Covenant; Abraham is ninety-nine and Ishmael thirteen when God institutes the rite of circumcision. By this time, Abraham seems to have settled into thinking Ishmael must be the promised child. And that's okay with him. He certainly wants the boy to live under God's blessing.

But now, *for the first time*, Abraham is specifically told that God will bless *Sarah*, that *she* is to be the mother of nations. "Change her name from Sarai to Sarah" (meaning "chieftain," "ruler," "princess"), God said, "for it is Sarah who will bear the promised child."[8]

Accordingly, it appears that Sarah knew nothing about her role as coheir of the covenant blessing until *after* Ishmael was born, and *only one year before* Isaac's birth. Even then, it was not her husband who told her. While eavesdropping on Abraham and his three heavenly visitors, she first heard the startling news. She could hardly suppress her laughter. To enjoy sex at her age? To have a son at this time next year? In view of what she knew about her own body—how wild!

But Sarah did conceive and give birth to the promised child. Now she understood: the unique blessing of God is on Isaac. So when she saw Isaac's position threatened by Ishmael, Sarah was fiercely protective. "Get rid of that slave woman and her son," she ordered her husband, "for that slave woman's son will never share in the inheritance with my son Isaac."[9]

Everything in Abraham protested Sarah's mandate. Ishmael was his son! He loved him dearly; how could he possibly send him away?

But did God tell Abraham to assert his authority and let Sarah know he is boss? Not at all. Instead, God said, "Listen to whatever Sarah tells you."[10]

The word "listen" is the Hebrew word *shama*, meaning "to hear intelligently," and it implies obedience. In other words, "Act on what you hear." Or, as the RSV renders this verse, *"Whatever Sarah says to you, do as she tells you. . . ."*

This story hardly illustrates the model of submission popularly preached today. What clouds the issue more is that God supported her.

I saw the issue was not Abraham's submission to Sarah, nor yet Sarah's submission to her husband. The issue was submission to the word of God—for it was God's word which Sarah declared. "Do what she says," Abraham was told, "because it is through Isaac your offspring will be reckoned."[11] Isaac, not Ishmael, was the heir through whom the Promise would be fulfilled. There was absolutely no alternative; the bondwoman and her son must go.

Did this mean Abraham was always to do Sarah's bidding? Of course not. In fact, when Sarah proposed Abraham have a child by Hagar, Abraham should not have listened to her. After all, he had a promise from God. But Sarah did not—not at that time.

It was different the moment she received power to conceive. Then she became a participant in the covenant blessing. Now, she, too, had a promise. She demanded appropriate action to assure Isaac would be the sole heir of his father. Ishmael was compelled to exchange his inheritance for freedom.

Much has been made of Sarah calling Abraham "lord," but "lord" was simply the common title of respect in that day. It is the same word Rebecca used when she gave Abraham's *servant* water, saying, "Drink, my lord."[12]

What is Peter's point? He wants it understood that Sarah was not putting her husband down. True, when she knew God's expressed will, she was not intimidated by Hagar, by Ishmael—who was at least sixteen—by her husband, nor by what the neighbors would say. Fearlessly, she declared what was right. At the same time, she called her husband "lord." As a godly wife, Sarah showed Abraham due respect.

"You are her daughters if you do what is right and do not give way to fear," Peter declared. In other words, "No matter what, you must fearlessly obey God." But this doesn't give a woman an excuse to lord it over her husband with some spiritual revelation—even when she is right. If a sure word from God means she must stand in opposition to her husband, God expects her to do so with gentleness and respect.

The express issue here is not who's boss in the family. The issue is submission *to God*. And Sarah's authority belongs to any child of God committed to doing what God says.

In sorting out the myths from the biblical record, we see Sarah in a new perspective. No more can we portray her as the unquestioning, blindly submissive wife. To do so is a distortion of truth.

Another thing. To commend Sarah's lying as indicating her obedience to her husband and her holiness is likewise outrageous. God did not commend her; in fact, her lying got her into serious trouble. It also brought tragedy and pain to many.[13]

What does the Bible say? "The Lord detests lying lips, but he delights in men who are truthful."[14] And it lists among those who will not be in heaven, "everyone who loves and practices falsehood."[15]

As for Sarah going along with Abraham's lies—we need to bear in mind that God put up with a lot of things in the Old Testament that He did not tolerate in the New. Clearly, He expected something more of those who had been exposed to the teachings of Jesus and had the light of the Gospel.

This is apparent in the story of Ananias and Sapphira.[16] When Sapphira parroted her husband's lie, did she get a pat on the back from Peter—or God? Hardly! The lie cost her her life. How, then, can we do that which God calls sin, and take refuge under the cloak of submission? We can't. To think we can is irrational.

Yet pulpit-pounders and typewriter-crusaders continue to make irresponsible statements that disregard the meaning of the original texts. Bent on defending their own personal preferences and self-styled opinions, they deny women the freedom that is rightfully theirs in Christ. For the most part, Christian women are afraid to challenge those who thus twist the Scriptures; they fear to be denounced as feminist, accused of being rebellious, or told they are the ones deceived. They not only fail to speak up, but many end up supporting the submissive model to assure approval.

A Personal Result of Distorted Submission

What happens when the headship-submission teaching is distorted? Let me share a letter from a friend, an R.N., a divorcée:

> Concerning the question you asked me on submission. Yes, it definitely was a factor in our problems. A year and a half before our breakup, I had been studying under Dr. N——, and this was his strong point. In a short time, I became almost opinionless and literally dumped all the decisions on Bill. If our communication had been good, we could have discussed this. He could have expressed how he felt, and some adjustments could have been made.
>
> In the belief that God would honor my submissiveness, I told my husband—and I meant it—that I would go anywhere or do anything that would help him in any way. I became almost a slave, and I couldn't understand why he was unhappy.
>
> About the same time that this was happening, women's lib was becoming strong, and Bill, being in management, was embracing the contemporary and feeling I should become more and more a career woman since the children were nearly raised. He said that I was becoming a nothing.
>
> Up to that point, I had planned to do nothing but be a housewife and the executive wife that required much travel and entertaining. But now, in a quick effort to please him, I began trying to get involved again in a choir and in nursing. But by this time, too many changes only added to the disturbance. . . .
>
> If I were ever to marry again, there would have to be a deep understanding of oneness not only in spiritual things, but also in our differences of opinion, so we could talk anything through and respect each other.

Now, I know some couples say that acting on the headship-submission principle has worked to make a bad marriage good or a good marriage better. But for others, like my friend writing on the previous page, the results have been disastrous.

It is easy to understand how a man, originally attracted to his wife because she was smart, competent, and decisive, feels betrayed when she "becomes a nothing." How drab a marriage when one partner never offers a stimulating idea or challenges the other's viewpoint! Even husbands who think they want to make all the decisions without challenge may find that this is not the sort of wife they want after all.

What happened to my friend is not an isolated case. Countless wives—and husbands too—who have sought to implement distorted concepts of headship-submission teaching in their marriages have ended up devastatingly disillusioned. The teaching practically guarantees that if a wife submits to her husband—no matter how unreasonable or cruel—God will honor her and bring her husband into a true role of headship, and the wife will have her "womanhood restored" and truly be fulfilled. But reality often repudiates the guarantee.

Because this teaching stresses that the success of a marriage hangs principally on a wife's submission, she subsequently bears the brunt of the burden when it fails. If she submits and nothing changes, or if her husband walks out, she still ends up loaded with guilt feelings. The upshot for shattered wives is bitterness, depression, and even suicide.

I know one wife who went the extreme submission route only to have her situation become so intolerable that she saw no other way out than taking her own life. But someone dared insist to her that she had no other alternative than to start obeying *God*. She did, and things began to change. A short time later her husband said, "I'm so glad you finally decided to do what God said to you."

We have to ask, too, whether or not a wife's unquestioning submission to a neurotic husband causes him to act responsibly. Common sense and observation say no. Instead, such unquestioning submission feeds his neurosis. And what of the wife who says, "By the time I submit to one order from my husband, he has changed and demands something quite opposite from me. I can't win for losing!"?

Then there is the woman who grabs at headship-submission: she wants her husband to tell her what to do, how to do it, and when to do it. She shies away from making decisions because she comes unglued when her choices turn out to be wrong. If her husband makes all the decisions, the blame is all his. She finds submission a welcome relief.

Submission can also be a spiritual cop-out. The need for daily personal encounter with God is shrugged off. Why bother to dig into the Word? Why bother to know God's voice if all of God's leading must come through one's husband?

Ironically, the idea of the husband as spokesman for God is held by many who denounce the Roman Catholic confessional on the basis of the scripture: "There is . . . one mediator between God and men [*anthropos*, the human race], the man Christ Jesus."[17] Yet they turn around and say that the husband is high priest in his home, therefore all divine orders must come through him; it is his sole prerogative to relay God's messages to his wife and family.

Every Christian must realize the significance of what happened to the temple veil at the moment of Christ's death. This heavy linen curtain was supernaturally ripped from top to bottom, proclaiming that *anyone* could enter the holy of holies—the presence of God. No more did one have to be a high priest to hear God's voice, to have intimate communion with Him. Many who teach headship-submission would, in effect, sew up the curtain and again exclude women from the intimate presence of God.

The Godly Wife of Proverbs 31

Proverbs 31:10-31 is a beautiful acrostic poem exalting womanhood. But it has not escaped mutilation to support the superficial Total Woman concept. I was appalled at the outrageous distortion appearing in one Christian periodical. A husband and wife had practically rewritten the passage, twisting the words to make obeisance and pampering one's husband the poem's message. The Proverbs' picture of the ideal wife and mother has much more to say about her excursion into the business world and ruling her household than it does about her homemaking—or pampering her husband.

What most of us overlook is that the first word of the poem concerns *the husband*. What is this spiritual leader's attitude toward his wife? Her husband "has full confidence in her." He respects her. He grants her the dignity of her womanhood. He trusts her implicitly to run the household, handle the finances, invest in and take charge of business operations. He not only allows her to achieve her full potential, but also trusts and supports her in doing so.

Obviously, this woman didn't run to the city gate to check with her husband about every decision she made. If she had, she couldn't have accomplished a fraction of what she did.

Let's take an honest look at the Proverbs lady: an intelligent and successful businesswoman, an industrious and efficient housewife, a volunteer social worker, an adored mother, a cherished companion; vivacious, healthy, physically and emotionally strong, beautifully dressed, commanding, a woman of wisdom.

Frankly, this woman's accomplishments leave me breathless. But the quality which makes the Proverbs lady of extreme worth is her *spiritual stature*. Above all else, she fears the Lord, and her awesome reverence for God affects every facet of her life. Because pleasing God is her first priority, she not only conscientiously rewards her husband's trust, but her life is genuinely fulfilling.

What About a "Covering"?

We hear much today of the need for Christians to be "covered" by some individual or group. The idea is that one is covered or protected by the one to whom he submits. We are told that such a covering is a *must* for protection from demonic activity, from Satan's attacks, and from deception. But when I go to the Word, I conclude that the teaching on "covering" must have been put together from fanciful conjecture.

Pastor James Beall, in his book *Your Pastor, Your Shepherd*, writes about "covering": "I find no precedent for such a practice in the New Testament. Paul, for example, never covered Peter, nor did Peter cover John."[18] And if there had been any such practice, surely it would have shown up in Paul's letters to Timothy, his son in the gospel. But Paul never suggests that Timothy offer him slavish obedience. Instead, he admonishes him to "be strong in the grace that is in Christ Jesus."[19] The number-one priority of every soldier of Jesus Christ is to please his commanding officer, he said. So, it wasn't Paul's approval Timothy was to worry about. Rather, Paul urged him, "Do your best to present yourself to God as one approved."[20]

Paul knew his death was imminent. But does he say that when he is gone Timothy will need to attach himself to some other minister in a covenant-relationship that will provide covering? Why would he? He had already thundered those freeing words, "There is . . . one mediator between God and men, the man Christ Jesus."[21] Paul had never set himself up as a go-between for Timothy in his approach to God. Nor would he ever put Timothy under that kind of bondage to any man.

Yes, Paul said that he had lived his life as an example for Timothy to follow. But he put the full responsibility on Timothy to guard the gospel and the gifts that had been entrusted to him: "Guard it with the help of the Holy Spirit who lives in us."[22] Timothy's *oneness with Christ* would enable him to carry out this responsibility, provide spiritual direction, and protect him from the Evil One.

There is a peculiar twist to this teaching on covering that defies logic. It says that a wife is covered or protected by submitting to her husband; as long as she submits to him, she is safe, under the umbrella of his authority. But the husband? He has to find someone *outside* the covenant of marriage to submit to—someone to give him advice and okay nearly everything he does.

This concept is full of problems. First, it denies what Jesus said about two people in a marriage covenant being "no longer two, but one."[23] It breaks up the basic unit that God ordained marriage to be. Together as one, a man and his wife were meant to order their lives before God in obedience and love. Their union did not include a third person.

And what did both Peter and Paul say about mutual submission? That all members of the Body of Christ—husband and wife not excluded—were to be in mutual submission to each other—irrespective of sex. We tend to forget that a husband and wife are also brother and sister in the Lord.

What's more, Paul said the privilege of sonship has nothing to do with being male or female. There are no distinctions that exist between those who are one in Christ. In a Christian marriage both have equal standing before God. If the wife has the same right of access and ability to hear from God, why would the husband need confirmation from an outside voice? The idea that he does is a perversion of truth and a snare to the marriage.

We also find, this concept denies what the Bible teaches about a married couple's unique capacity to hear from God. We have the promise that if any two are agreed on earth, it shall be done.[25] Surely no two persons have greater potential for spiritual agreement than husband and wife; their prayers of mutual accord should be especially effective.

There is a catch, however. Peter was very specific: Husbands, if you don't treat your wife with respect, if you are not her loving protector, if you don't recognize that you and your wife together are fellow heirs of God's gracious gift of life, don't expect your prayers to be answered. But if your attitude is right and you treat her as you should, you can talk to God, and He will answer.[26]

Why, then, does the husband need to form a covenant relationship with some man in order to hear from God and get His directions? He doesn't.

There is no reason why a husband and wife together cannot seek the will of God about every detail of their life. God is committed to respond with guidance. My husband and I can attest that it works. Time after time when we have faced decisions, God has shown us separately and together His choice for us. This includes major moves, what house or what car to buy, as well as going here or there, doing this or that. Nothing that concerns us is too insignificant to receive guidance from the Lord about.

One passage of scripture invariably referred to by those who argue for covering is the statement of Paul's concerning propriety in worship:

> The head of every man is Christ, and the head of the woman is man, and the head of Christ is God. Every man who prays or prophesies with his head covered dishonors his head. And every woman who prays or prophesies with her head uncovered dishonors her head. . . . A man ought not to cover his head, since he is the image and glory of God; but the woman is the glory of man. . . .[27]

This means, we are told, that the veil was a sign of subjection. Therefore, a woman is covered by being in subjection to her husband. This "principle" is then somehow stretched to mean that all men need to be covered by being in subjection to some other man. It seems that any method of interpretation can be used if it fits someone's preconceived ideas.

In her scholarly book, *The Bible Status of Women*, Dr. Lee Ann Starr points out that at the time the Apostle wrote, the unveiled head was a proclamation of harlotry; the veil, the badge of a virtuous woman. But if one claims the veil is a badge of subjection, this is what follows:

1. (a) The veil is a badge of subjection.
   (b) A wife should be veiled to show she is in subjection to her head—her husband. . . .
   (c) The husband should not be veiled; thereby showing that he is not in subjection to his head—Christ.

Again:

2. (a) The veil is a badge of subjection.
   (b) The woman who prays or prophesies, wearing this badge of subjection, honors her head—her husband— by acknowledging his authority over her. . . .
   (c) The man who prays or prophesies, wearing this badge of subjection, dishonors his Head—Christ. He must not acknowledge the divine authority over him.

But the expositors assure us that the veil is also a badge of humility:
   (a) A woman must wear a veil to show that she is humble.
   (b) A man must not wear a veil; he is not humble.

Dr. Starr concludes, "The Apostle's logic is awry or expositors have misinterpreted the veil."[28]

As for the verse, "For this reason, and because of the angels, the woman ought to have a sign of authority on her head,"[29] expositors agree it is one of the most difficult passages to interpret in the entire New Testament. Dr. Starr protests that the words "a sign of" are not found in the original text, and that the Greek word *exousia*, translated here "authority," is translated elsewhere as "right." Furthermore, Thayer's Greek-English lexicon gives the first definition of *exousia* to be "the power of choice" or "the liberty of doing as one pleases." "For this cause ought the woman to have *right* over her head" means that the woman ought to have the power of choice or the liberty of doing as she pleases in the matter of veiling or unveiling. She is only constrained by doing that which will bring honor to her husband and bring no reproach on the Christian community.[30]

Could we say, then, that man-made coverings are an attempt to play God? God has said that He himself is our protector. Note what the psalmist says:

> He who dwells in the shelter of the Most High
>   will rest in the shadow of the Almighty. . . .
> *He will cover you* with his feathers,
>   and under his wings you will find refuge;
>   his faithfulness will be your shield and rampart. . . .
> If you make the Most High your dwelling—
>   even the Lord, who is my refuge—
>   then no harm will befall you. . . .[31]
> (Emphasis mine.)

The task of keeping His own safe, Jesus put into the hands of His heavenly Father.[32] And who knew better than Paul the reality of God's keeping power? With absolute certainty he declared, "The Lord is faithful and he will strengthen and protect you from the evil one."[33] He assured us that if we make our requests known to God with thanksgiving, "the peace of God . . . will guard [our] hearts and minds in Christ Jesus."[34]

When pressures come, and hazards stalk men and women of spiritual daring, James Beall points out that it is the significant phrase "in Christ," found throughout the New Testament, that makes all the difference. He writes:

> Coming into Christ is far more important than most church people realize; it is the difference between life and death. . . . Paul tells us that as part of our conversion-initiation experience of entering in at the door, we receive our covering. . . . *Those who*

*insist on a man-made covering fail to understand the inheritance
we have already received in Christ—a covering so complete that
it is inconceivable that it could be supplemented.*[35] (Emphasis
mine.)

In fashioning man-made coverings, we court the same spiritual disaster that Paul tried to head off in the Galatian church. Foolishly these fairly new Christians had listened to "false brethren" pedal a "different gospel." And they were about to reinstate the bondage of custom and tradition, thus denying the all-sufficiency of Christ. Paul went right to the heart of the matter: "You are all sons of God through faith in Christ Jesus, for all of you who were baptized into Christ have been clothed with Christ! There is neither Jew nor Greek, slave nor free, male nor female, for you are all one in Christ Jesus." [36]

What reason is there then to exalt the creature above the Creator by casting mere mortals in roles of "spiritual protector"? It is Christ who has triumphed over all spiritual adversaries! The believer's victory comes not from sitting under another man's umbrella, but from being "clothed with Christ," and from continually abiding "in Christ."

Does this mean we do not need leadership or pastoral care or that we do not need to submit to the counsel of our pastor? Far from it. But in guiding us, God's anointed leaders will concern themselves with our being servants of Christ, not slaves to them.

The key to right relationships in the home and the church is mutual respect and mutual delight in serving one another. True submission is not passive acceptance but positive action. As Jesus laid down His life for us, so are we called to lay down our life—"our rights"—for others. If we are clothed with Christ and continually abide in Christ, we won't be fighting an incessant battle for "my rights." In Christian love, we will yield our preferences, putting our mates' or our Christian brothers' and sisters' wants and needs before our own.

While submission also implies a teachable spirit, we still need always to watch out for any devious use of the Scriptures in what we hear. Because there *are* unscrupulous teachers, Paul admonishes believers to "test everything," and "hold onto the good." [37] If we don't, we may be hoodwinked into believing we are being obedient to the Word, while in reality we are committed to error. And we could end up in shackles under the guise of submission, instead of enjoying the priceless freedom that is ours in Christ.

6

Who's in Charge Here? Submission Gone Haywire

The frightful news surged through our community, leaving a wake of grief and stunned disbelief. Pastor Hammon was dead. Convinced he was healed, and determined to trust God, he had stopped his insulin injections—and died in a diabetic coma. Mavis Hammon, at thirty-three, was left a widow with five young children.

I didn't know the Hammons, but from friends and relatives scattered throughout our area, I learned grim bits and pieces of the bizarre tragedy. Then came another jolt. Mavis, along with Kirk Kruger, a friend of the Hammons, was being charged with involuntary manslaughter. What I heard of the particulars left little doubt in my mind that the Hammons had been victims of deception. But I knew only Mavis could explain how this could have happened, so I prayed that the Lord would bring us together. He did. Mavis bought the house we were renting, and we moved just down the street!

The more I got to know Mavis, the more I was sure that she was not guilty. Her life was marked by openness, honesty, emotional stability, and just plain goodness, along with her sturdy faith and solid commitment to Christ. There had to be extenuating factors. I suspected that given the same circumstances, many Christians would have made the same tragic mistakes.

When I spoke to her about telling what had happened, she readily agreed. "Matt and I were ignorant of this sort of deception," she said, "and Christians need to be warned."

Because of the personal nature of the events, I have changed names and some unimportant details. Otherwise, here is the Hammons' story just as Mavis told it to me.

It all began when Kirk Kruger walked into Matt's office at the church. He was a new Christian, he said, and had come to the pastor because he was eager to grow spiritually. Matt was thrilled to meet someone so excited about the Lord. He knew Mavis would be delighted to meet this dynamic young man. When she did meet him, she was just as impressed as Matt was with Kirk's enthusiasm and zeal.

Kirk started coming to the Hammons' home in the evenings, often talking until one or two o'clock in the morning. He spoke candidly about his first marriage ending in divorce; his present wife lived in another state; he had been named top salesman for a large corporation; he had been into TM, ESP, Mind Dynamics —whatever gave him power over others upped those sales. But now he wanted help to grow in the Lord.

"At first we were glad to spend time with him," Mavis told me, "but as the weeks went by, staying up night after night left both Matt and me exhausted. As a busy pastor and psychologist, Matt had a heavy counseling load. Also, other circumstances had contributed to this period being a low point in our lives—making us more vulnerable to Satan's attack. Even our children were beginning to resent our spending so much time with Kirk."

Kirk seemed to think he could learn through counseling sessions what Matt had learned through the experiences he'd had while walking with the Lord for many years. He was looking for a quick way to spiritual maturity.

As the months passed, other things about Kirk began to bother Mavis. Why was he always wanting to burn candles? And, why did he become so upset when Matt was unable to relax and let his mind go blank as Kirk sometimes insisted he do?

There was one incident Matt related to her which had left her particularly uneasy. It happened one night, very late, after Mavis had finally gone to bed. Matt was in the kitchen, Kirk in the bathroom directly opposite the kitchen. Suddenly, the light in the kitchen began to glow brighter and brighter. It became so intense, Matt flipped the switch off.

When Kirk came out of the bathroom, he asked Matt why he had turned the light out. Matt said, "Because the light got so bright I couldn't stand it."

Kirk was elated. "It worked!"

"What worked?"

"Concentrating in the mirror—it caused the light to brighten."

Mavis had growing feelings of distrust. "I wondered if some things Kirk told us were true or just made up to take up our time." But when she shared her misgivings with Matt, he wouldn't listen. Nor would he listen to close friends who kept warning them that they were being taken in by Kirk.

Kirk's powerful, persuasive personality seemed to have both Matt and Mavis in control. "We were fine when he wasn't around," Mavis says, "but this wasn't often. I never had a chance to talk to Matt alone. And when Kirk was there, it seemed as if Matt and I were doing only what Kirk told us to do."

One night the Hammons attended a healing service in a nearby church. Matt, who had been on insulin since his teens, went forward and knelt at the altar to be anointed with oil for the healing of his diabetes. Throughout the next few weeks he felt that he had been healed, though not completely. But Kirk insisted that Matt *was healed*, and should stop taking his insulin.

Close friends reminded the Hammons that sometimes God heals slowly; perhaps Matt should merely cut back on his insulin. This made sense to Matt and Mavis, but Kirk said that was nonsense since Matt was healed. Kirk talked about the devil putting "symptoms" on a person even after he is healed. Though a diabetic's diet can be a matter of life or death, he told Matt, "You should eat everything, and *feed your doubts.*"

This troubled Mavis. "I felt this was presuming on God. Still, we were puzzled about what to do. Following the healing service, Matt did not take insulin for five days. The few times he tested his sugar level, Kirk got very upset."

Matt's behavior began to be marked by confusion. One minute he would say he felt he couldn't trust Kirk, the next, that the Lord told him to trust Kirk for his healing. Friday, he came home upset with Kirk and the church staff, and his sugar was high. At 3:30 p.m., he gave himself an injection of twenty units of insulin, but immediately berated himself for doing so.

Mavis knew something was wrong. But what?

Around midnight, Matt spilled out the problem. That past Monday morning Kirk made him promise God not to take any more insulin without first calling Kirk to pray with him.

This shook Mavis. "To me, vows were serious. *You just do not make vows to God and then break them.*[1] I never had any reason to doubt Matt's relationship to the Lord. If the Lord was telling him to trust Kirk, then Matt would have to trust him—though Matt didn't know why and neither did I."

Matt decided to tell Kirk what he had done. Kirk insisted Matt renew his vow, but Matt resisted. Finally, Matt took Kirk back to his room and told him to get out of the car. He wouldn't, so Matt drove home and they sat in the driveway arguing. If Matt wouldn't make the vow again, Kirk said that he would lay on the horn and wake everyone up. In the end, Matt again made the vow—and Kirk agreed to go home.

Saturday afternoon, Matt's condition worsened, and he went to find Kirk. While he was gone, Mavis hid his insulin—he couldn't take it because of his vow to God, she reasoned. When she and Kirk refused to let him have it, he told Kirk to leave or he would call the police. In the scuffle that followed, the phone was pulled off the wall.

Matt also made a vow not to go to the hospital until he passed out. Kirk left, and Matt went upstairs to explain to the older children why he had reacted so; he was like a drug addict—without the insulin his body needed, he became frantic. He thanked Mavis, too, for taking it away so that he couldn't break his vow again.

Around ten-thirty Saturday night, Matt began to get very sick. Mavis was beside herself with fear. She went to get Kirk since he had no telephone. "If Matt had promised to pray with Kirk before taking any insulin, I felt I had to get him quick." Mavis knew Matt belonged in the hospital. But when Kirk arrived, there was no mention of the hospital. "He took over, and I did just what I was told."

Sunday afternoon, Matt, suffering intense pain, called Mavis and said that the Lord told him to take seven-and-a-half drams of wine. The Hammons never had wine in the house, so Mavis dashed to the neighbors to borrow some. After Matt took the wine, the vomiting stopped and the pain eased off.

That evening Mavis wanted to take Matt to the hospital, but Kirk said, "No!" Mavis seemed helpless to do anything.

About three-thirty in the morning, Matt seemed to be resting peacefully. Kirk told Mavis to go to bed. He would lie down on the couch in the living room. . . .

Mavis struggled awake and looked at the clock. Oh, no! It was 7:25, and she was late getting up to get the children off to school. At least Matt must still be sleeping, thank the Lord for that. She would check on him first . . . "Oh, God—no!" She wanted to scream.

Numbly, she called Kirk. "Send the children to school, but don't say anything to them about their father," he ordered.

Somehow she stumbled through getting them fed and out of the house. Then she went back into the bedroom to pray. Mostly, she felt mad—mad at God. "God, You can't do this to me!" she sobbed. "You have to bring Matt back . . . We trusted You . . . You promised . . . God, Your reputation is at stake! . . . You have to make this right. . . ."

She wanted Kirk to call the church office and ask the prayer chain to pray that God would raise Matt back to life. He refused.

About 1:00 p.m., the doorbell rang. It was Joella, the Hammons' baby-sitter, inquiring how Matt was. Mavis wanted to tell her the truth, but Kirk warned, "Don't tell her anything!"

"Why can't I?" Mavis persisted.

"There was this man who had a rare blood disease, and people thought he had died when he hadn't. Maybe this is the case with Matt. We have to have faith."

As the hours passed, Mavis became more distraught. "What should we do?" she pressed Kirk.

"What do you mean, what should we do?" he shot back.

Mavis decided it was out of her hands. "I couldn't do

anything," she told me.

When the children came in from school, Kirk told her to have Joella take them out for supper. They left about an hour-and-a-half later, not knowing their father was dead.

As soon as the children were out of the house, Mavis confronted Kirk. "I don't know what to do. But we have to do something!"

Kirk picked up the phone and dialed the police rescue squad. When they arrived they called for a coroner and the police. Mavis waited in the living room while Kirk led the police into the bedroom. When they came out, the sergeant said he would put the death down as suicide.

Mavis protested. "No way was it suicide!"

But Kirk silenced her, saying that it was only a technical term.

She wasn't able, however, to put the policemen's comments from her mind. What exactly had Kirk told them? Beset with the feeling that she had to know, the day after the funeral she drove to the police station. What she heard was even worse than she feared. The tears stung her eyes as she drove home, hurt and angry. But surely the police believed her—or did they?

A couple of weeks after she had taken her children and gone home to her mother's, Mavis received a call from friends. The D.A., they said, had announced over the news that the police were looking for her and Kirk. The newspapers were carrying the same report. Mavis was stunned. There was nothing to do, of course, but to get in touch with the police at once.

A few weeks later, a grand jury charged Kirk and Mavis with involuntary manslaughter and ordered them to stand trial—together. Both were declared guilty. For eight years Mavis lived under this threat daily until the State Supreme Court acted on her appeal, finally reversing the guilty verdict, and completely exonerating her.

When I talked with a Christian psychologist about the Hammons, he said, "This is a good account of a psychological 'master' over two persons who became his psychological 'slaves.' There is evidence of the demonic, too.

"Actually, it would have been easier for Matt to have risen

from a coma and gone for help than for Mavis, with her background and temperament, to have broken out of her role as 'slave' and asserted control.

"But don't think only submissive personalities become caught in this trap. Satan can bind a dominant person through someone with a 'controlling spirit' too. Indeed, college-trained professionals can become psychological slaves—I've seen it!"

Obviously, if we are to protect ourselves from this sort of bondage, we need to understand what is involved.

A "controlling spirit"—the tendency to control others—can be a characteristic of the human spirit, it can be demonic, or it can be a combination of both. Individuals who exhibit a controlling spirit go beyond simple manipulation to wield a phenomenal mastery over another person or persons. The takeover may be fast or slow, but it is always subtle. The controlling individual monopolizes an unsuspecting person's time, asserts control over his close associations, sways his thinking, and directs his decisions. Without realizing what is happening, the victim becomes the psychological slave under the control of the psychological master.

Even though the master-slave phenomenon can transpire solely on the human level, there is strong indication that evil spirits were at least partly behind the coercion and control responsible for Matt's death.

One aspect of Mavis' personality did undoubtedly play a part in what happened. Although she is quiet, shy, and unassuming, Mavis is quick to respond to another's needs and she would never want to hurt anyone's feelings. She says Matt was equally compassionate. That is why neither of them confronted Kirk about disrupting their family life and monopolizing their time. Thus, unwittingly, they gave Satan an advantage. Had they heeded certain precautions, the tragedy could have been prevented.

Most Christians know less about these safeguards than did Mavis and Matt. And unless informed, they are just as susceptible to this same sort of deception. What are the warnings she would sound?

1. Do not let another person tell you that you are healed;

always go to a doctor for confirmation before stopping medicine.

2. Beware of psychic phenomena, and be on guard against anyone who is or has been involved in parapsychology (ESP, clairvoyance, telepathy). These can lead to deception by Satan.

3. Be cautious around persons who are very persuasive, especially those about whom you know little.

4. Beware of the techniques taught by salesmanship organizations, especially those including hypnosis and mind dynamics.

5. Never let a third person come between a husband and wife on any matter. Be especially careful of a third person whom one partner does not trust.

6. Guard your home and family from persons who play on your sympathy and disrupt your home life. Your first responsibility is to God, then to your family, and after that to others.

When I read over these warnings, a series of pictures flashed to mind—other people I know who could have avoided tragedy or at least averted painful problems had they observed these safeguards.

Master-Slave Phenomenon in Leadership Training

Gene Church's book, *The Pit*,[2] presents a very clear picture of the extent to which this principle can be taken. Though extreme, the techniques used are not uncommon.

The Pit is the nightmarish account of a group of executives who, in the interest of making it to the top as salesmen, became virtual prisoners in a four-day encounter session. Participants in the training session said that they were obliged to attend in order to get ahead in the company.

The book reads like a description of concentration-camp horrors, rather than an experience in group dynamics. The students were physically beaten and whipped, psychologically battered, forced to act in degrading ways and to perform unnatural sex acts, and to submit to being stuffed into coffins, and "crucified" on a cross. The idea was to rid them of their hangups, and force them into complete honesty. For this they paid one thousand dollars each.

It was obvious and unquestioned that the president of the company was the undisputed leader. "We felt, when we arrived, that by following his example and submitting to his leadership, we might become better leaders ourselves," Church says. "But during the class, something went awry. The element of violence was introduced in bizarre and macabre fashion. Students found it futile to resist, futile to try to escape, futile to speak . . . an example not of how foolishly men will follow, but how completely men can lead. We felt, when we arrived, that by following his example and submitting to his leadership, we might become better leaders ourselves."[3]

It appears that the leaders made the most of the master-slave phenomenon. It is disturbing to consider that the students under the spell of these leaders themselves acted out a large part of the violence and macabre punishments against each other. One is left with the haunting question: What sort of leaders and salesmen does such training produce?

To a lesser degree, the intense training programs used to teach people how to manipulate others into buying an item, whether it is needed or not, are of the same nature. For example, it is one thing to sell a housewife a good dictionary or a set of books based on need; it is quite another thing to do it via mind control.

Who cannot remember buying at least one item from a high-pressure salesperson which we did not really want to buy at that time?

Controlling Spirits in General

If you're thinking, "Not me! I'd never let anyone take over that kind of control!" don't be too sure. One need not be weak or dim-witted to end up a psychological slave. A boss can become the psychological slave of his secretary, an employer of his housekeeper, a counselor of his counselee, a friend of his friend, even a parent of his child, and any one of us of a person we are trying to help—if that person has a controlling spirit.

I saw this happen to a charismatic teacher who at one time had positively influenced my walk with the Lord. His marriage was destroyed, his ministry shambled, when he let himself fall prey to the control of his secretary. At the time he turned his back on his wife and children, he said it was to give himself more fully to his ministry—ignoring the scriptural teaching that his wife and children were his *first* ministry.

Knowing both the husband and wife, I felt a particular sadness. The wife had sought a reconciliation with her husband "for the sake of the children and the gospel." But the husband was not interested. By then it was no secret—he had fallen for his secretary. A friend close to the situation told me, "That woman has a controlling spirit. And the control she exercises over —— is incredible."

One control tactic she used was seeing that messages sent from husband to wife, and wife to husband, often did not reach the other partner, causing one crisis after another. (There are many ways for a secretary to assume a controlling role—and for the devil to get into the act.)

To be sure, there were other difficulties as well in this couple's marriage. But the possibility of working them out was clearly undercut by the control the man's secretary wielded. Satan did a masterful job of deception and destroyed another ministry.

A Controlling Spirit Among Shepherding Ministries

It would be nice to think that every pastorate is filled with those shepherds whose one aim is to care for the needs of the local body of believers. Unfortunately, the problem of pastors' misuse of their position has intensified. Certain facets of the current renewal have made Christians extremely vulnerable to the master-slave phenomenon. The heightened tension and pressure of ordinary daily living is such as to produce a disposition easily imposed on by controlling persons.

Where do these pressures come from? And how is it they engender the master-slave roles?

The pressures come from two sources. First, from a hedonistic-materialistic society pushing the individual's need to "be fulfilled," according to its view of fulfillment. We are told that prestige, prosperity, and pleasure are the ultimate.

The second pressure comes from Christians at large. This is the pressure to "be spiritual." We are bombarded with the notion that spirituality can be measured in terms of prestige, prosperity, and pleasure (happiness and healing). Christians are hard-driven to up their positions, up their incomes, and up their blessings.

Frazzled by the push to be fulfilled and to be spiritual, men and women are easy prey to erroneous teaching on discipleship, shepherding, headship, authority-submission, or whatever offers an end to the struggle. Under the circumstances, the distorted concepts sound so good. Total submission to one's spiritual "head," be it husband or shepherd or whoever wields authority, relieves all responsibility. Follow orders and don't worry. If the person who handed down the order is wrong, he has to answer to God—not the person who did as he was told. Or so the lie goes.

Exhausted from chasing a phantom ideal, all too many relinquish personal responsibility to mentally gasp: "Yes, yes! make my decisions. Tell me what to buy . . . how to spend my money . . . whom to marry . . . what to do with my kids . . . how to handle my affairs. . . ."

"Submission" becomes an escape, a way out of having to wrestle with hard decisions.

Do not read me wrong. We do need counseling and guidance from those over us in the Lord, but it is a lie of the devil that advocates blind obedience and says that we are not responsible for our final decision. Furthermore, when anyone continually makes personal decisions for us which we ourselves should be making, psychologically, he becomes our master and we become his slave.

It's true, people become psychological slaves, or inappropriately subservient to others for reasons other than "spiritual" submission. But the dynamics are much the same.

Warning Signals of the Master-Slave Phenomenon

When reading Gene Church's book, *The Pit*, one is caught up with the pulsating question: Why would anyone allow himself to be so tyrannized? When Church attempts to answer this question—an answer he stresses is a complex one—I'm struck by how similar the factors he elucidates are to those I've heard spelled out by others who have escaped religious cults—including individuals who had been entrenched in discipling and shepherding groups which demanded absolute submission to the leader or group. What were they? Financial commitment, fear tactics, group pressure, sexual exploitation, fatigue, and denial of reality. Let's look at the similarities.

1. *Financial commitments.* Church's assertion that the thousand-dollar fee was a binding factor underscores the saying, "To gain control of an individual's finances is to gain control of the individual." It works the same way for those who have made a considerable investment of finances or properties in a religious group. It is simply not easy to walk away.

2. *Fear tactics.* The use of fear tactics and group pressure within religious groups is common. I knew a family who were members of a pyramid shepherding group for seven years. During that time, everything they did was dictated by those over them. They never went to the bank without permission, never made a phone call unless absolutely necessary, never met with other Christians outside their group.

I met the wife when she came for counseling. Nine months earlier, the family had left the shepherding group physically and geographically, but emotionally, psychologically, and spiritually, they still struggled to be free.

Fear of criticism, fear of rejection, and fear of punishment which controlled them while in the group were cruelly extended when they left. God's discipline was prayed upon them. They were told that they were being given over to Satan for discipline, that they would no longer hear Christ speak, that they were finished in the ministry. Group members who happened to meet them were not allowed to speak to them. The fear tactic was employed to force "the rebellious ones" back to the shepherding church. These pressures plus Satan's accusations wield a powerful force for control of the mind.

3. *Fatigue.* A prime factor in accepting the witless and cruel behavior of the group, says Church, was fatigue. Fatigue is an effective device used by many cults to gain control. Former members of People's Temple related how Jim Jones kept them in a

state of perpetual exhaustion; the pattern was three or four hours sleep at night. Fatigue so distorted their thinking and broke down their defenses that they accepted beatings as right and good. Mavis Hammon, too, attests to the dire effect of exhaustion.

4. *A sense of unreality.* Like Church, those who escaped the People's Temple holocaust also spoke of a sense of unreality which rendered them helpless. Again, Mavis could only attribute her irrational behavior to a sense of unbelief that what happened could happen.

5. *Sexual exploitation.* Sexual exploitation can figure into the psychological takeover of an individual. Church reported sexual exploitation in the forced participation in debasing sex acts. Sexual exploitation of members by religious cult leaders is common knowledge; sex with whomever of his following he might choose is the leader's right, he claims. But this sort of abuse can also happen in the church—yes, in orthodox, evangelical, and charismatic circles.

Some years ago, a friend—a new Christian at the time—narrowly escaped being preyed upon by a popular evangelist. In telling me what happened, she said, "No one ever told me there were false prophets in the Church. And I thought he was a powerful man of God."

Slick at ferreting out new converts, this man claimed revelation to lure young women to meet with him privately. "He wanted to talk to me, he said, because God had revealed to him something very precious about me. I was to come to his headquarters in a large evangelistic truck, and he would tell me how God was going to use me," my friend remembers.

And so she went. When she got there, the police were swarming everywhere. They had been tipped off by the mother of a fifteen-year-old girl. She had been lured to the truck on the same pretense of revelation, only to be taken advantage of sexually.

Sexual exploitation is not always so blatant. In subtle ways, Christians sometime violate the sexuality of others to gain control. A man may capitalize on the concept of male dominance to manipulate a woman to cater to his every whim. And a woman may capitalize on the concept of the female dependent role to gain attention and cunningly manipulate control.

6. *Pride.* Pride is the single most contributing factor to the master-slave phenomenon. Pride is the driving force behind a controlling spirit, and pride is the snare by which one becomes a psychological slave.

A plea which in essence I hear again and again goes like this: "I tried to help Val, but now I'm the one who needs help. She calls at all hours, keeps me on the phone forever, often insists on seeing me at once. Or she may show up at my door and stay for hours on end. She's driving me up a wall. And I don't know what to do!"

Why is it that most of us can't handle this sort of problem? Because we take pride in being the nice guy, pride in being a caring person, pride in always being available, pride in being known as a spiritual advisor. We would never put it into words, but we really see ourselves as Val's "savior."

With such an image to protect, we dare not confront Val, because to do so would destroy the image. This is self-deception. Pride and delusion keep us subjugate to the "Vals" in our life.

Pride also makes us easy prey to the apple-polishers. The Bible tells us that silver and gold are tested in the crucible and the furnace, "but man is tested by the praise he receives."[5] Paul warns us to keep away from those who "by smooth talk and flattery . . . deceive the minds of naive people."[6]

Of course, praise may be the genuine expression of an appreciative heart. Or, again, it may be the strategy of those who "flatter . . . for their own advantage."[7] In either case, our response will be determined by whether or not we are wholly set on pleasing God—even at the cost of displeasing those who matter most to us.

It is sad when a minister has been overpraised and his ministry turns into an ego trip. In this case, both the person and ministry become extremely vulnerable to deception. What follows will likely be a new teaching or "revelation."

Sometimes Christians stay locked in a slave bond simply because they are too proud to say, "I was wrong." They publicly committed themselves to a group or followed after some renowned leader or championed some strong teaching. The day comes when they begin to see the error and realize that they have been deceived. But pride keeps them from admitting their mistake, so they go on pretending. Not only do they remain a slave to the deception, but worse, they cause the deception to spread.

There is a way out. Jesus said, "The truth will set you free."[8] By humbling oneself and speaking the truth, the captive can once again walk in freedom. Daring to speak the truth can also bring release to others.

If you have surrendered control of your life to some individual or group, know that God wants you free to be controlled by the Spirit. Every detail of our life is to be under the Holy Spirit's control. Understand, though, that Spirit-controlled men and women are not limp, floppy puppets maneuvered by strings. Rather, they are persons to whom the Spirit communicates God's will, and who determine to do God's will at any cost. Not in their own strength, but empowered by the Holy Spirit.

On the other hand, those who have been playing God, manipulating situations or people, need to abdicate their man-made kingdoms—whether one individual or many persons are involved. Jesus said, "The rulers of the Gentiles [pagans] lord it over them, and their high officials exercise authority over them"[9]—but His people are not to be like that.

Our will—the power to choose and to determine our action—is God's gift to us. We have no right to surrender it to any man; God does not even ask us to surrender our will to Him. To give up our rights, yes, but surrender our will, no. Only when the power of conscious and deliberate action remains ours can we say with any validity, "I delight to do thy will, O my God."[10]

Learning to recognize God's will in the myriad interpersonal relationships that life affords isn't easy. But it is essential if we're to be kept free of bondages He never intended for us.

Appropriate submission to those in biblically designated authority roles involves freedom to choose; one *chooses* to submit—but only in ways the Bible holds forth as fitting. Subjugation to inappropriate authority involves the loss of freedom; one slavishly knuckles under out of fear—no matter how improper the demands.

How thankful I am for the many spiritual teachers and Christian friends who have counseled, rebuked, encouraged, exhorted, and deepened my understanding of God and His kingdom. But my gratitude is the greater because they dared to trust the Holy Spirit in me. They haven't tried to usurp control by subtle manipulation or by illicit claims of authority. Rather, they let me learn and grow by making my own decisions—right or wrong. Best of all, they love and accept me even when my choices are faulty.

We really don't have to try to be the Holy Spirit in another person's life. Nor do we have to come under bondage to someone "more spiritual," letting them control our lives. Not when we stand firm in our faith that God is worthy of all our trust—and His Word declares: "He guides the humble in what is right and teaches them his way."[11]

7

Being Friends—But Free

Total commitment to the lordship of Jesus Christ clearly involves a commitment to love—not love as some mushy, sentimental feeling, but love that respects individual personality and responds to need. But most of us have discovered to our dismay that in actual life situations, *commitment* to love does not solve all the difficulties. Sometimes we simply do not know the appropriate response, the loving thing to do. Conflicts do erupt, even in our closest relationships, which can leave us hurt, frustrated, angry, confused—and terribly guilty. We may smile and say that everything is fine, only to end up bitter and resentful. In any case, problems in our ongoing personal relationships can woefully disrupt our spiritual progress.

It is not only conflict which poses a problem. One can also come under bondage in one's relationships because of a false concept of what Christian love requires.

How well I know! A few years ago I found myself entrapped and nearly devastated by some very complex and troubling relationships. Even after God clearly showed certain steps to freedom, the inner conflicts were not immediately resolved. I found it difficult to reconcile what was happening with what I had been programmed over a lifetime to believe *should* happen. *Love hadn't conquered all.* Consequently, I was gripped by terrible guilt.

A question gnawed at my mind: *Is it possible that we expect our interpersonal relationships to conform to a religious ideal-model which is unscriptural and unrealistic?* If so, this is deception, and deception will always bring us into bondage.

Suspecting this was the case, I turned to the Word. I wanted to know: *Are all negative feelings or reactions toward another Christian sinful? Does the concept of "perfect love" leave any place for maintaining certain "distant" relationships by virtue of individual preference? Are we obligated to seek, develop, and maintain close personal friendships with all Christians with whom we have frequent contact?*

These questions were birthed out of my own bitter experience; scriptural answers were crucial to my spiritual healing. I share this time of my life at the risk of reproach, praying that God will use what happened to me to show how Satan works to lock us into spiritually disastrous relationships.

Let me start at the beginning.

I was a newcomer in the community when Jean had reached out, welcoming me into the prayer group that met in her home. When her aged mother moved in with Jean and her family, we rented her mother's house only a block down the hill from Jean's. Close neighbors, we became even closer friends. Scarcely a day went by that she did not stop by for coffee.

"It's so quiet and peaceful here," she would say.

"You mean with five kids, their gang of friends, a stream of college students, and visiting relatives, it's not quiet at your house?" I would banter. "How strange!"

Naturally, I often walked up the hill. Being alone all day, I enjoyed the buzzing activity of her household. However, I was soon aware that Al resented our being together so much. One day Jean was with me when he came home for lunch and again when he came home from work at five. The moment she was out of the house he exploded, "Seems to me you'd have something better to do than just sitting and talking all day!"

"Jean hasn't been here *all* day," I shot back. "Anyway, she's having a rough time handling her feelings about what is happening to her mother. Being in this house with all its memories is very important to her just now. She was born in this house, grew up, and was married here too. . . . This house represents all she feels is slipping away—forever.

"Can't you understand that? Or don't you ever care about anyone else?"

Because I felt guilty, I meant to make him feel guilty too. But Al was absolutely right; I didn't have that much time to be idle.

Still, I enjoyed Jean's company, so we went on as before, always finding something interesting to talk about. Though one thing did bother me. If I took issue with her on any matter, she was immediately defensive. If we did discuss differences of opinion, too often I ended up feeling like a small child being patted on the head. One day I brought up the controversial subject of movies on campus. Bravely, I plunged in.

"I can't believe some of the movies being shown in the college chapel!"

Her smile was indulgent. "You couldn't possibly understand the field of education. If we are going to have a liberal arts college, they do have a place."

I didn't agree. But what could I say?

I was so concerned with protecting our friendship, I was not even free to be myself. Jean's dominant personality, her academic background, her position on the faculty, her strongly held opinions, and my deep feeling for her as a friend—all led me to sidestep issues that might lead to conflict. I did so even when I believed something to be morally wrong. And because I didn't want to risk losing her friendship, her approval or disapproval inevitably affected my response to God's leading. In no other relationship had I ever encountered such a problem. I did not know how to break the bondage, and if I had known how, I did not have the courage.

Problems which developed out of this relationship spilled over, with a dire effect on an already troubled marriage. The tension from constant conflict, along with the fear of an upcoming surgery, decreased my ability to handle pain. At the time, I didn't recognize these contributing factors. I honestly thought the problem was mostly physical, so I desperately downed prescribed pills, trying to get relief.

Subconsciously, I was bent on destroying myself because I

saw no other way out of the dilemma. At the conscious level, I didn't want to die; I just wanted to stop hurting. Somewhere in between, at a nonverbal, semiconscious level, I was making a desperate plea for attention. In effect, I was shouting loudly, "Please, can't somebody do something? I can't take any more—the pain or the problems!"

One day, to make my point, I emptied the bottle. The chaplain with whom I was associated called in the doctor who worked closely with him. Since I needed rest badly, he gave me a tranquilizer, something different. But not many hours later, I began to experience the same side effects which had nearly ended my life four years before. It was the jolt I needed. No more tranquilizers; I didn't dare.

For three months, there were days when the pain was so intense, my tongue thickened, my mind clouded as if I had overdosed. Ragged patches of time would be torn from that whole year.

At the same time God was working in my life concerning submission and authority. Adjusting my attitudes and actions accordingly sparked disagreement between Jean and me. Because no one else can know exactly why we make certain responses or choices when there are personal and family problems, my actions were often misread by her. Other times, unquestionably, I acted unwisely.

A minister friend, meanwhile, graciously attempted to help with a family problem which seemed hopeless. To me, he was a godsend. I had carried this particular burden alone for so long. Now someone was saying, "Here, let me carry the burden for you." Someone I could trust, someone I could lean on, was paying attention and caring.

But what was right and good came to include an element that was wrong. What was wrong was an illegitimate attempt to meet a strong personal dependency need. Unknowingly, I was looking for a person to meet a need which only God could meet.

About this time, a letter came from a friend. Before I finished reading it, I was trembling. He said, in part:

The Old Boy invariably hits us at our points of greatest weakness.

I sense that you have a great hunger for human love and that it is extremely difficult for you to let Jesus himself fulfill all your needs. If that is true, you can be sure Satan knows it; he will be out to exploit it.

Be very careful, particularly . . . keeping that relationship [with this minister] exactly as the Lord would have it. You have been called to a hard walk, harder than most. But He never calls us to a cross greater than we can bear. So few are willing to give their utmost for His highest will—don't disappoint Him, Florence. . . .

Perhaps, if my defenses had not been up so at the time, I would have recognized that God had prompted the writing. Instead, I was baffled and hurt.

Although Jean did not understand what I was going through, she sensed I was deeply troubled. Not wanting to hurt her, I simply tried to back off; I desperately needed breathing room. She told me later how she felt I was "pushing her away." But, she said, the Lord told her to keep reaching out to me, and to keep praying for and with me.

Perhaps He did. Maybe the Lord was trying to squeeze me into such a tight corner that to be free I would have to make a deliberate break. But in spite of feeling I was being smothered, I had not quite come to that place yet. It is not easy to break off a friendship when one is already struggling with feelings of rejection—and loneliness.

This was no easy time for Jean, either. Despite the hurt and confusion she felt, she tried her best to turn things around. When I read the note she sent expressing the wish that "we could again be close," I felt numb. Several times we tried to talk through the problem, but it only grew worse. I felt she never really heard me.

That we could both love Jesus Christ and be committed to Him, and still have this breakdown in communication seemed utterly incongruous and terribly unspiritual. That I did not want to be close again heightened the guilt feelings.

What was wrong with me? If love and forgiveness were real, why couldn't there be a restoration of our relationship to the way it was before? Deep inside, I knew it was because I had to be free to stand up for what I believed was right and to determine God's word to me without pressure from anyone. I saw no way out of my dilemma.

That whole miserable year, I was torn between the desire and need for acceptance and companionship, and the urge to escape when there was conflict. I still did not realize that physical pain was not the whole problem; I needed to be set free from the bondage of these relationships, but subconsciously I blocked out this need. To have faced up to it would have meant that I must do something about it. And that was frightening—for how could I reconcile such action with what *I thought* God demanded of me?

Even when we subconsciously block out the Lord's voice because we really don't want to hear what He has to say, He still has his own strategy for getting through! And so He did—quite unexpectedly, in a psychology course I was taking.

That day, Dr. Floyd McCallum was lecturing on "relationships." Suddenly all my senses were keenly alert. My fingers tightened on my pen, and I was conscious of my own deep breathing. God was speaking through Dr. McCallum directly to me.

As I listened, I saw an instant replay of the whole preceding year-and-a-half. In that same instant, I was flooded with amazingly clear insight. Now I understood why, during those desperate pain-riddled days, I was unrestrainedly swallowing pills.

Dr. McCallum explained: "We do have a psychological impact on each other. . . . The company we keep nurtures that which is predominant in our personality. A domineering friend will cause a clinging vine to become more clinging, more dependent. A clinging vine will cause a dominant friend to become more domineering. . . ."

Then these words came like the thrust of a sword: "Some of you had better break certain friendships because the people you are associating with are dragging you down emotionally." And he added, "I feel led of the Lord to say this!"

I closed my eyes against the rush of tears. "Oh, God, You *do* want me to be free!" The sudden release was overwhelming.

It was clear to me now. There were numerous pressures I had been trying to escape—the physical pain, the conflict in the home, more than one hurtful relationship—which increased the tension and frustration and left me loaded with guilt. When I saw that my fear of rejection affected my obedience to the Lord, I almost did myself in. All these things compounded had been more than I could handle.

How could it happen? Did not Scripture promise: "God is faithful, and he will not let you be tempted beyond your strength, but with the temptation will also provide the way of escape, that you may be able to endure it"?[1]

I had my answer when I saw what I had not noticed before. It was the "therefore" signaling a contingency relationship between what has gone before and what immediately follows. And what follows here? Paul's injunction: "Therefore, my beloved, flee from idolatry."[2]

—But wait. Paul was writing this to the Corinthians. Corinth was filled with pagan temples. I was no idol worshiper—or was I?

The truth was that for a short time God had slipped from first place in my life. I did not think so then. But *we can get into bondage to a person or thing which, in a sense, becomes a god.* Securing the esteem and acceptance of another person had at times taken preference over my having God's approval. Idolatry! no less.

And that made me vulnerable. No wonder when Satan maneuvered a squeeze play, I went down in a heap. Only when we order our lives with the singleness of purpose to please the Lord and not people—when we flee idolatry—are we assured God will not allow us to be overwhelmed by temptation.

Following that confrontation through Floyd McCallum, God made one thing very clear. The ministry to which He has called me demands that I be free to move in obedience to His direction at any time, without having to consider a friend's reaction.

This does not mean that I do not need spiritual counsel from God's appointed leadership or brothers and sisters in Christ. I count such counsel absolutely necessary to keep *me* from deception. But God has called me to walk with even the closest friends held loosely. At the same time, He has called me to become involved with many individuals in their deepest hurts. The struggles He allowed me to go through have better equipped me to handle these relationships.

Precautions We Need to Take

I found that in order to avoid conflict and bondage, the dynamics involved in one-to-one relationships cannot be ignored. I found that before trying to force any relationship to conform to the "religious ideal-model," we need to know what God's Word does *not* say, as well as what it does say. Moreover, in order to build up one another in love, we need to grasp something of the Holy Spirit's working within each individual in interpersonal involvement. We need to remember, always, that both persons involved in a relationship are equally important to God.

Simply knowing that interpersonal relationships greatly affect our relationship to God and our physical, mental, and emotional well-being is not enough. We need to be alert to potential hazards and pay attention to some basic rules. Though with some friends we are apt to think no guidelines are necessary, still we can be drawn into a difficult situation before we realize it. It is much easier to get into such a spot than to get out of it. Let's set out some guidelines.

1. *Jesus Christ must be central.* We need to submit every relationship to the lordship of Christ *before* becoming deeply involved. We should ask Him: How am I to relate? And, to what extent? Following the Lord's nudges and checks will result in much less friction and far more fulfilling friendships.

2. *Awareness.* In this whole matter of relating to others, the word is not *suspicion* or *aloofness,* but *awareness.* Every relationship contains inevitable elements of conflict, disagreement, and misunderstanding, but their occurrence does not have to devastate either party nor destroy the relationship. Our awareness of the dynamics, the dangers, the basic rules—and that God puts our lives together for His purposes—will help us to structure right relationships according to biblical principles and keep us free from unscriptural demands.

It is essential to our understanding that we see that we do relate to different people in different ways. With some friends, even though we seldom spend time together, there is a special feeling of closeness. With others, we can be together a great deal, but never feel especially close. Some friendships will flourish through our whole life. Others are warm and fulfilling only for a time.

Accepting that not all friendships are alike and that there are shifts in how we experience closeness will allow us to relax the demands we make on ourselves and others.

Consider, too, that we are not today the people we were yesterday. We change in knowledge, understanding, spiritual perception, and awareness. Someone who meets our need today may not do so tomorrow. We may fill a special place in another's life, but for a limited time only. Life is a process, and with the ongoing changes, our needs vary.

The breakup of a friendship for any reason is never easy. It can be excruciatingly painful, but the pain may be eased if we accept the fact that life is not static, and recognize that God walks people *through* our lives for a purpose. *A friend is not a possession.*

3. *A willingness to let go.* We need to learn to let go. Why do we find this so difficult? Why do we cling doggedly to a relationship which is no longer meaningful, needful, or which may have become emotionally devastating and spiritually stifling? Most of us were taught to think that as Christians we must; our obligation to love and unity allows us no alternative. Just wanting to back off a bit makes us feel guilty.

But suppose we were to find something wrong with our friend, some devilry, some vice. . . . If we can't find something wrong, we are likely to provoke hostility, subconsciously hoping that our friend will react badly enough so that we have the legitimate reason we need—or think we need—for breaking off the friendship.

One thing for sure, few of us would dare say that God wants us to end a close relationship, or that we believe this is the right thing to do. Who would buy that! But those who are sensitive to God's voice will find God does indeed direct us on occasion to break off friendships. I am not talking about an angry falling out, but God may want to dissolve a relationship for any one of several reasons. There can be forgiveness and healing and love without necessarily resuming the same close association as before. I know, because Jean and I have experienced this.

Why should God direct that we put some distance between us and a Christian friend? It may be because our too-closeness prevents us from new experiences and the learning that would come from them. Or, a too close relationship could prevent our learning dependence upon the Lord and to know His voice for ourselves. It could hinder our growing up and becoming our own person—free to come under the rule of Jesus Christ. Or, perhaps, the Lord just wants to give the friendship a new direction.

4. *Realize our personality limits.* Though we might wish it were otherwise for Spirit-filled Christians, the uniqueness of our personalities limits the adjustments we can make to one another. We need to see that though we love and respect someone, we may not be compatible. If we could accept this inevitability and act accordingly, many hurts could be avoided. And there would be far fewer battle scars among the saints.

One of the most fruitful missionaries I know says with a twinkle, "God says I have to love everybody—He doesn't say I have to work with everybody."

5. *Only God can resurrect.* If we do not understand what is happening, guilty feelings may cause us to try to pump life into a broken relationship to bring life back and to heal. But only God can resurrect what is dead. And perhaps in this case He does not want to. Of course, if the breaking off has been caused either by our being hurt or by our inflicting hurts or both, there must be forgiveness. Forgiveness sought; forgiveness given; forgiveness received. There is no alternative.

Though the Lord may not want to restore the relationship to the same form it had, invariably He wants to heal the hurt and the scars. His will is always for the two individuals to come to peace with themselves and with each other. And there can be mutual respect and acceptance—at the same time letting the other go free.

Susceptible Areas to Interpersonal Entanglement

Yesterday, as Jean and I talked over this chapter, she noted, "Isn't our purpose in friendship to *be* not to *have* a friend?" It is. And getting involved with individuals, relating beyond the superficial, is the norm of the Spirit-filled life. Yet there are limits to our *capacity* for close relationships.

Sometimes we may be the only meaningful person to become involved in the struggles of another. If so, we are particularly vulnerable to manipulation and bondage. The relationship may become a security blanket for the one we are trying to help—for us, something more akin to a ball and chain. Up till now this person's problem has been having no one; our problem becomes the inability to give out to anyone else.

Obviously, this sort of situation is more problematic for certain people. Pastors often find themselves encumbered by former parishioners who won't give them up but go right on hanging on after the pastor has left one parish for another.

Christian counselors know the burden that can ensue. I have found myself in this difficult position after having reached out to someone to whom God wanted to channel His love or speak a word through me. God worked uniquely in one divine moment, but the person assumed I had a continuing "special" ministry to them. This might be true, more likely not. And future demands on my time and strength were impossible to meet.

Teachers have a similar problem. Having spent a great deal of time with a student during a particular crisis, the teacher is threatened by the student's desire to become a lifetime project.

Young people do have terrific problems, and teachers need to be available, but even the most dedicated can handle only so many student relationships. When attention is shifted to someone else who needs help, the first student sees it as rejection. He may react with anger or depression, consciously or subconsciously, employed as an attempt to reestablish that relationship. It takes real strength and wisdom to refuse to be manipulated and yet to be supportive from a new distance.

Signs of Being a Psychological Parasite

Most of us would not plan to get entangled with an individual who is a psychological parasite—someone who feeds on the psyche strength and emotional structure of another. But it can happen without planning when we take on far more responsibility for the other person than we have the right to assume. Then to our dismay, we find they cannot go anywhere, do anything, or make any decision without us.

A few individuals encourage such attachment because they enjoy the attention. We all need to be needed, but the psychological parasite caters to an exaggerated need to be needed. And sooner or later, when the demands become excessive, an explosive reaction is almost sure to occur. How can we tell if we have unknowingly become attached to someone in an unhealthy way? Sudden apparently inexplicable hostility might be one sign that we have become a parasite. Another indication, if we are hurt when someone close slips off alone without us, subtly hinting that he or she needs more breathing room.

We have no right to make anyone feel he must include us in his plans. Nor do we have a right to monopolize anyone's time, stealing one of his most valuable possessions. While we may think we are God's gift to a friend, too much of anything lowers its value. Solomon recognized the problem and said bluntly: "Let your foot rarely be in your neighbor's house, lest he become weary of you and hate you."[3]

Invariably, a person living at the psychological and emotional expense of another forges reciprocal bondage. To throw off the shackles, the dominant friend needs to refuse to make the other's decisions or to have his time encroached upon. The psychological parasite needs to grow up. Taking the responsibility for making our own decisions will keep us from becoming a psychological parasite. And acting responsibly will also keep us from allowing someone else to drain off our energies and usurp our time—unless God so directs.

Love Involves a Risk

Most of us learn early that every relationship has its risks and its rewards; that hurt or fulfillment is experienced only to the extent of involvement; that the more we love, the more we can be hurt. And because we learn this the hard way, who of us has not said at some time, "Forget caring relationships!—I'm taking no more chances on getting hurt"?

These feelings may follow one deep heartbreak or they may build up from our having suffered through several hurting relationships. If a relationship has been a disaster, it is natural to withdraw. We are sure we can never reach out, never open up to others, never share ourselves again.

The truth is that we can, because when we determine to do

what pleases God, we can expect Him to "work in us both to will and to do his good pleasure."[4]

' And, "because God has poured out his love into our hearts by the Holy Spirit, whom he has given us,"[5] the Spirit will enable us to express agape love in real and practical ways. Involvement will never be without risk. But we can count on the Holy Spirit impregnating every relationship we submit to the lordship of Christ, effecting spiritual fertility and growth out of both the hurts and the fulfillments.

When the Holy Spirit worked to bring my relationships under the lordship of Jesus Christ, it was a breaking experience. But out of the brokenness came tremendous release. No longer do I have to try to fit my interpersonal relationships to a religious ideal-model that is neither realistic nor scriptural. I am aware of the dynamics, the dangers, and the basic rules to help me relate to others in ways the Bible clearly directs. And I've made the joyous discovery: *agape* love is without bondage.

God walks people through our lives for a purpose. We all need warm, caring relationships. But we dare not allow ourselves to become locked into a relationship that in any way thwarts our spiritual growth, or renders us hesitant or ineffectual in carrying out the Lord's orders.

When we allow God to put our lives together as He wills, He alone can pull all the strings at once. Try as we might, we cannot manipulate our interaction with others to effect our greatest good and His greatest glory.

Our loving heavenly Father not only can, He can for *all* concerned.

8

"The Next Voice You Hear . . ."

A question I hear asked over and over again is: How can we recognize God's voice? The question is crucial for two reasons. First, if we miss hearing God when He speaks, we cannot obey His directions. Second, if we think we hear God speak, but the voice is not His, we can be deceived into disobeying God's will. In this case, the words we think God is speaking may rise from our own human spirit. Worse, we may be fooled into thinking Satan's voice is the voice of God.

A spiritual hearing problem of any kind can get us into all sorts of trouble. But Larry's tragic death is a grim example of just how deadly the deception can be when a person mistakes Satan's voice for the voice of God.

The story begins on the night before a three-day winter conference where I was to speak. Having flown in from Buffalo that afternoon, I sank back in the cushioned softness of my chair, grateful for this quiet evening to relax. There were four of us in the room: conference director, John Kimlingen, two young people on his staff, and I. John and I were exchanging past experiences, talking about the ways we had seen God work. When we came to the subject of deliverance, I said that sometimes when I am in the presence of demonic powers, I get a sharp pain in my head. It doesn't happen every time, but whenever it does, I know exactly what I am up against. Now note, because of what happened later, that at no other time that weekend did I mention this to anyone.

On the last day of the conference, as I shared about the heavy dealings of God in my life, all over the room the Spirit began to surface haunting memories, long-standing hurts, deep resentments, unforgiveness, hidden sins. For more than four hours we ministered to men and women who came forward for prayer.

Among these was a young man I guessed to be about nineteen. John slipped an arm around his shoulder. "Florence, this is Larry. He's been hearing a voice—God's voice, he says. But he says he can't do what God is telling him, because he's so full of fear. He wants to be set free from this fear."

John's look carried a warning; so did his words as he went on. "The trouble is, that he won't tell us what this voice is saying. About six months ago, he said God told him to do this." He pointed to a scar where a cross had been cut deep into the boy's forehead. He had ended up in a psychiatric ward.

I studied Larry's face. Pudgy cheeks, full lips, blond hair neatly trimmed, his eyes on a level with mine, darting, haunted. I had noticed him during the service.

"Is John your pastor?" I asked gently.

"Yes."

I explained to Larry that because of his spiritual immaturity and lack of knowledge of Scripture, it was imperative he tell John what this voice was commanding him to do. "All the voices which seem to be are not from God."

"I can read the Bible. I can tell God's voice!" he shot back.

"Can you?" I drilled in. "Do you know that the Bible says the cutting of the flesh is an abomination to God?"

"No." He looked startled.

"Well, if you would have checked with your pastor first, you wouldn't have ended up in the hospital in that mess. We just don't take any voice that comes along. God's Word tells us to test all things by two or three witnesses."[1]

Not to be dissuaded, he insisted we pray for him to be delivered from the fear.

"No," I told him. "I won't pray for you unless you are willing to surrender your independent, rebellious attitude. Rebellion, the Bible says, is like the sin of witchcraft.[2] Unless you first deal with the rebellion, you will only end up worse off than you are now."[3]

I found myself speaking to Larry with increasing forcefulness. This confirmed what I suspected: the Spirit of God within me was confronting the Enemy. Yet, it was unsettling when Larry picked up on my aggressiveness. Backing up a step, he muttered, "Don't get mad at me."

"I'm not mad. But I am concerned, because I feel this *is a matter of life or death.*"

I sensed that it was desperately important, so I continued to urge Larry to tell John what this voice demanded of him. And twice again, I stated emphatically this was no game, but a life-or-death crisis. The last time, Larry turned as if to walk away. His voice dropped. "I just don't want you to worry about me."

"Worry about you? I'm not worried, but I am concerned."

He shrugged. "Well, I just don't want you to get a headache."

I caught my breath hard. "*What did you say?*"

"I don't want you to get a headache."

"Why did you say that?"

He looked bewildered. "I don't know."

Meantime, John had turned aside to speak to someone. I stepped over to him. "Do you know what Larry just said to me? *He doesn't want me to get a headache.*"

"Of course, that's not him talking," John said.

"I know. But I don't know whether or not to tell him."

John nodded. "Yes, we'll tell him."

He spoke kindly but firmly. "Larry, you couldn't possibly have known this, but Florence told me that at times she reacts with a headache in the presence of demonic powers. You've opened yourself to some religious spirits, and you think you are hearing God's voice."

Larry indicated no surprise at the problem, only at the way it had been exposed. Again we pressed him to tell what the voice was saying, but he hedged, "I have to think about it."

As we continued to work with Larry, I realized that although he wanted to escape from the inner terror, he was neither willing nor ready to take the necessary action that would break the grip of the powers of darkness that held him captive.

Five weeks later, John called. "You remember Larry? . . ."

"I surely do."

"Well, *he's dead*."

John explained that the police had found Larry's body on the edge of a pond. Stripped naked except for four religious medals, Larry died of exposure after "baptizing" himself. Apparently, religious spirits bent on destroying him drove him to this outlandish act.

As John told me what happened, I could hear Larry stubbornly insisting, "I know God's voice," and the Holy Spirit's warning, "This is a matter of life or death." As I hung up the phone, deep inside I heard the Lord say, "It may not always be so dramatic. But just remember, whenever you minister my Word, it is always a matter of life or death!"

I would never forget it!

The Case of King Saul

Most of us think, "Not me! I'd never fall for such a trick of the devil." Pointing to Larry's immaturity, his previous involvement with drugs, his subsequent mental and emotional state, his lack of knowledge of the Word, and his unteachable spirit, we would be quite right in saying, "He was easily deceived."

Yet who was it to whom Samuel the prophet said, "Rebellion is like the sin of divination, and arrogance like the evil of idolatry"? None other than Saul, king of Israel!

Saul's portrait stands out in sharp contrast to the fragmented, troubled Larry. Handsome and towering head and shoulders above everyone else, Saul was "without equal among the Israelites." Yet when Samuel let him know that on him rested "all the desire of Israel," he demurred: "Why do you say such a thing to me? I'm the least of the least!"[4] Nevertheless, the same day Saul was anointed king, the prophet's words were confirmed as the Spirit of God came on Saul in power and prophecy. He had been handpicked by God.

At this point in Saul's life, we would be far more likely to nominate him "man of the year" than to compare him to someone like Larry. But a look at the overall record shows striking parallels.

Saul's ruin began when he failed to retain his humility, a

prerequisite to the Spirit's presence and power. Again and again he put his own judgment before the Lord's. To begin with, he usurped the priestly role to offer the sacrifice which Samuel was to offer. Then, when God commanded Saul to totally wipe out the Amalekites and everything belonging to them, he decided, "What a waste! Kill the people and the scrubby cows, yes—but not King Agag and the fat calves and choicest sheep."

But sheep will bleat and cattle will low. Samuel, hearing the cacophony, wanted to know why. "I obeyed the Lord," Saul assured him, "but the soldiers saved the very best sheep and cattle to sacrifice to your God."[5]

Samuel's eyes blazed. "Does the Lord delight in burnt offerings and sacrifices as much as in obeying the voice of the Lord? To obey is better than sacrifice. . . ."[6]

Saul found that God is not impressed by sacrifice intended to appease disobedience. And more, God's judgment is sure. "Because you have rejected the word of the Lord," Samuel declared, "he has rejected you as king."[7] Saul's rebellion had cut him off from God's voice. Never again while Samuel lived did God speak through him to Saul.

Incredibly, after Samuel's death, Saul again sought to sidestep God's judgment. He went to the witch of Endor and demanded she bring Samuel from the grave. But Saul's hope for a reprieve was soon dashed. The prophet passionately spelled out Saul's doom: Disobedience and deception had already cost Saul the kingdom and his family dynasty. Now it would cost him and his sons their lives.[8]

Saul and Larry shared two death-dealing attitudes: *pride* and *rebellion*. Saul, headstrong and self-willed, refusing the prophet's counsel . . . officiating as priest in offering the burnt offering . . . saving the best of the plunder and thinking to appease God by his sacrifice . . . cut off from hearing God speak, but determined to hear Samuel's voice even if it meant going to a witch in direct defiance of God.

—And Larry, arrogant and stubborn, refusing the guidance of his godly pastor . . . offering a "pagan sacrifice" by cutting his flesh . . . not heeding the Word—ignoring Christ's example in submitting himself to John for baptism, and the fact that nowhere in Scripture are we told to baptize ourselves . . . listening to spirit voices . . . determined to do his own thing and allow no one to stop him.

The end for both? Demonic torment and an untimely and tragic death. Clearly, whether we be a "king" or a "commoner," pride and rebellion throw open the door to Satan's suggestions and make any one of us a prime candidate for spiritual calamity.

Humility, a teachable spirit, knowledge of the Word, and absolute obedience to the revealed will of God according to Scripture—all are absolutely essential to keep us from being fooled into thinking Satan's voice is the voice of God.

Satan's Use of the Printed Page

Satan does not always *speak* his lines; he is quite adept at getting them into print. One trick which has served him well is to persuade Christians that "devotional material" containing spiritual-sounding phrases interspersed with loosely paraphrased Scripture is supernaturally inspired. In truth, such material may not be from God at all. The source may be merely human intellect. Or it may be a clever fraud by the Master of Deception.

A serious Christian would never consider attending a séance. Yet, many read the sort of material mediums receive through spirit séances or automatic writing—believing the origin is God. Two good examples are the books *God Calling* and *God at Eventide*, edited by A. J. Russell.[9] I recoil everytime I see them for sale among religious books. Thousands of copies have sold. And the unwary saturate their minds with these writings, believing them to be messages from God. I find, however, much to indicate the origin is, rather, a deceiving spirit.

The books were allegedly written by "Two Listeners"—two women who remain anonymous, who sat silently with pencils in hand and waited to get guidance such as A. J. Russell reported in his book, *For Sinners Only*. This practice of "listening" for "guidance" was commonly practiced by the Oxford Group, later to become the Moral Re-Armament movement to which Russell belonged.

In the preface of *God Calling*, one of the "Listeners" tells how she was "curiously affected" by Russell's book. A growing and persistent desire to get similar guidance led her to arrange to share a quiet time with the friend with whom she was living. From the first, her efforts were totally fruitless. But not so with her friend. "Beautiful messages were given to her by our Lord Himself, and every day from then these messages have never failed us."[10] She never received guidance unless the two were together, and then the messages were always communicated through the friend. Since Russell informs us that "not one woman but two have written this book,"[11] it appears that the friend must have acted as a medium.

My introduction to these two books came through a college student living in our home. Cheryl had received *God Calling* as a gift. It grew on her, she remembers. After two years, reading it had mostly replaced her Bible reading. Many of the passages ran through her mind like a tape recorder playing day and night. She, too, tried to get into total silence . . . to "listen" . . . to "hear a Voice" . . . to get "Guidance." Then a peculiar thing happened.

Traveling by bus, Cheryl met a lady from England. Not only was she delighted to have a seatmate who eagerly talked about the Lord, but one with an Anglican background—Cheryl is Episcopalian. She soon discovered another common interest—books. When Cheryl spoke of how much she treasured *God Calling*, the woman gave a stern reproof. The book was cultic, demonic. She must renounce it, pray for forgiveness and for release from its influence—they prayed accordingly—and she must burn the book along with her copy of *God at Eventide*.

Arriving home, Cheryl came into my office obviously upset, brandishing the books and wanting to know where she could burn them. Curious, I wanted to know what books and why. I suggested she leave the books with me. I'd look them over and let her know what I thought of them.

As I read the books, I was appalled. How could anyone claim these words were those of the living Christ? How could any intelligent person reading the book believe such a claim? Even if it did not violate the Scriptures, which it surely does, the claim would have been absurd. The book is filled with messages that are murky and obscure, like a picture out of focus.

During the next few weeks, Cheryl continued to be plagued with condemnation over these books. It took counseling and much prayer for her to be released from its influence.

The Book "God Calling" Under Analysis

What about the content of these messages purported to be given to these "two poor, brave women . . . courageously fighting against sickness and penury . . . today, here in England, by the Living Christ Himself"?[12]

Sometimes a quick tip-off to a cult or false teaching can be nebulous references to the Holy Spirit. By this, I mean exactly the sort of statements we have here:

> All work here is accomplished by My Spirit, and *that* can flow through the most humble and lowly. *It* simply needs an unblocked channel.[13] (Emphasis mine.)

> Listen quietly. Sometimes you may get no message. Meet thus all the same. You will *absorb an atmosphere.*[14] (Emphasis mine.)

Remember now, the Two Listeners claim the above are the words of Jesus. But would Jesus speak of the Holy Spirit as "that" or "it"? Never! When Jesus spoke of the Spirit, He was distinctly named—the Holy Spirit, the Comforter, the Paraclete (one who walks alongside to help)—a Person.

What is meant by "absorbing an atmosphere"? Some sort of spiritual osmosis? Hardly what the Bible teaches. It is the Person, the character, the words of Jesus which we are to receive, not an atmosphere.

Also sounding an alarm are the many positive references to the "Spirit-World" and "Spirit-Kingdom"—especially this incredible charge:

> Trust in the Spirit Forces of the Unseen, not in those you see.[15]

I wonder what "Spirit Forces" the Two Listeners saw? No matter. Since the Bible states that we are to have nothing whatsoever to do with spirits, but to trust only in God, I must reject this message.

Granted, the writer of Hebrews seems to say that those

heroes-of-faith who have died now surround us as "a great cloud of witnesses." But he does not say we are to direct our attention to them. Rather, in view of these witnesses, he charges, "Let us fix our eyes on Jesus."[16]

Perhaps the most significant passage for evaluating the book, and surely one of the most dangerous, is this:

> How often mortals rush to earthly friends who can serve them in so limited a way, when the friends who are freed from the limitations of humanity can serve them so much better, understand better, protect better, plan better, and even plead better their cause with Me.
>
> You do well to remember your friends in the Unseen. Companying with them, the more you live in this Unseen World, the gentler will be your passing when it comes.[17]

Do these sound like words from the God who commanded His people to have no communication with the dead, and decreed that those who did should be put to death?[18] The prophet Isaiah flung the question in the face of a nation who defied God in this matter: *"When men tell you to consult mediums and spiritists, who whisper and mutter, should not a people inquire of their God? Why consult the dead on behalf of the living?"*[19] To do so, he says, is to turn from light to darkness and death.[20]

When God created us with the potential to love and fellowship with Him, He didn't make us spooks. He created us to hear, taste, smell, see, and touch. How contrary to His intention, then, is this message:

> Your five senses are your means of communication with the material world, the links between your real Spirit-Life and the material manifestations around you, but *you must sever all connection with them, when you wish to hold Spirit-communication.* They will hinder, not help.[21] (Emphasis mine.)

It strikes me that if we were to "sever all connection" with our five senses, we would be in a trance, unconscious, or dead! And what sort of "Spirit-communication" is meant? Though God is Spirit, communication with Him is not something spooky. God and I communicate when I read His Word, gaze at the exquisite beauty of a rose, listen to the pounding surf of the ocean, taste the crisp tartness of an apple, smell the approaching desert storm. No, these experiences enjoyed through the senses are not, *in themselves*, direct communication with the Divine. But what God has so wondrously created for me to enjoy through my physical body stirs me to praise Him, to talk to Him. We do communicate, and without my taking leave of my senses.

Of course, in Christian meditation we communicate with the Divine through our spirit and mind. But even so, our intent is not to lose touch with the real world.

Just as ridiculous a message is this bit of nonsense:

> Endeavor that others may never see you anything but rested, strong, happy, joyful.[22]

How totally out of touch with reality! Jesus let His disciples see His tears. And Paul made sure that the church at Corinth knew there were times he despaired even of life. He knew how important it is that we share our pain. "Don't only rejoice together," he said, "but weep with those who weep."[23]

Another passage is this:

> Fight fear.
> Depression is a state of fear. Fight that too. Fight. Fight. Depression is the impression left by fear. Fight and conquer . . . fight and love and win.[24]

That is not only bad theology, it is bad psychology. Anyone who has suffered a deep depression knows the futility of trying to fight fear. The Bible does not say, "Fight fear"; it says, "Fight the good fight of faith."[25] Trying to fight our fears only tightens their grip and/or pushes them deeper into our subconscious. God's way of dealing with deep-rooted fear is through His love. "Perfect love," He assures us, "drives out fear."[26]

At first I wondered that the "Guidance" received by these women included this warning concerning their prayer times together:

> The devil will try by any means to stop them. Heed him not. He will say evil spirits may enter in. Heed him not.[27]

But then I realized that if Satan was the source of these messages, he well might say, "Don't pay attention to anyone suggesting you are in danger from evil spirits." On the other hand, God's

Word points out the very real possibility of satanic intrusion. So He tells us to "test the spirits," not to ignore them.[28]

Although I have quoted only brief statements, they are enough to refute the claim by these two women that the "living Christ" is the source of their writings. I suppose the incompatibility of these messages with the Scriptures, however, could be easily shrugged off by anyone who expresses such a casual view of the Bible as this:

> We felt all unworthy and overwhelmed by the wonder of it, and could hardly realize that *we* were being taught, trained and encouraged day by day by HIM personally, when millions of souls, far worthier, *had to be content with guidance from the Bible*, sermons, their Churches, books, and other sources.[29] (Emphasis mine.)

Keys to Knowing God's Voice

Don't think for a moment that I question God speaking to a person in the here and now. I know He speaks to me—not audibly, but nonetheless real. Sometimes the Holy Spirit implants a thought or idea in my mind. Or He may quicken a portion of Scripture to me. At other times, He speaks deep within my spirit in distinct words.

How do I know it is God who speaks?

I wish there was a categorical answer to the question of recognizing God's voice. The problem, of course, is that we are dealing with subjective experience and not objective data. The "inner voice" cannot be checked externally or verified by others. True, we can assess the results if we obey the voice we hear. But even then, while the outcome might prove it was *not* God's voice, the outcome does not necessarily prove that it *was* God speaking. Fortunately, there are guidelines which can help us to know the difference.

1. *Familiarity.* We learn to know God's voice in the same way we learn to know any human voice—by familiarity with the person.

Before I knew Al well—long before we married—when he called me on the telephone, he would have to identify himself to me. Now, thirty-six years later, when Al phones me, does he tell me who he is?

I suppose a gifted mimic could imitate my husband's voice and fool me. But I don't think anyone could keep up the bluff for long. I know my husband too well—I know how he says certain things and that there are some things he would *never* say.

In similar fashion, through the years I have come to know God: through His "letter" to me—my Bible—and through my ever-deepening relationship with Him. Consequently, I've learned there are some things God would never say. He will never speak at variance with His written Word. If He speaks through a specific verse in the Bible, what I take it to mean must agree with the whole counsel of God. This is why you and I dare not just dip into the Scriptures for what suits our fancy, and why it is so important to *study* the Scriptures.

What's more, any personal word I hear must never take precedence over the Bible. Nor should I regard God speaking in a conversational manner as a more elevated form of guidance than guidance from the Bible—as do the Two Listeners.

To sum up the matter, intimate communion with the Lord is not something apart from the Scriptures. We simply cannot separate the living Word from the written Word. If you think otherwise, consider David's stirring acclamation:

> The law of the Lord is perfect, reviving the soul. The statutes of the Lord are trustworthy, making wise the simple.
> The precepts of the Lord are right, giving joy to the heart.
> The commands of the Lord are radiant, giving light to the eyes.
> The fear of the Lord is pure, enduring forever. The ordinances of the Lord are sure and altogether righteous.
> They are more precious than gold, than much pure gold; they are sweeter than honey, than honey from the comb.
> By them is your servant warned; in keeping them there is great reward.[30]

Neither can we separate the Holy Spirit from the written Word. Any inner suggestion which is not in 100 percent agreement with the Word of God is not from the Holy Spirit. Satan is much too smart to hand us an obvious lie. Ninety-six percent truth and four percent error is more his style. We are much more apt to swallow a lie which is hidden in a large amount of truth.

2. *Be totally honest with yourself and others.* What about the inner voice that directs us to go to a certain place, speak to a particular person, or do a specific thing when there is no way to judge the content by Scripture?

I know of no other way to learn God's voice in these instances than through trial and error. Inevitably, we will sometimes make mistakes. When we do, the important thing is to be honest and simply say, "I was wrong." If we ask God to teach us from the experience, He will. This makes for spiritual maturity.

It is possible, of course, that we hear God correctly, but misinterpret the message. For instance, I know of three completely unrelated situations where three different men prayed for someone sick, each one believing God promised healing in the words of Malachi 4:2: "But unto you that fear my name shall the Sun of righteousness arise with healing in his wings. . . ." In each case, the sick person died, and those who thought these individuals would be healed were stunned. Later, each one said the same thing. They hadn't understood at the time that God meant healing would come through death. By "healing in his wings," God was indicating that it was the soul "in flight" which would be healed.

I have no reason to doubt that, in these instances, this is what happened. Still we need to be careful. If we have been wrong and then try to rationalize or explain away our blunders, we will never learn and will make ourselves candidates for bigger mistakes.

3. *Never become passive.* What about a conscious effort to turn inward to silence, to meditation, as a way to encounter God and to hear His voice?

To be sure, it is difficult to hear God speak while we are a ceaseless, churning entity of planning, brooding, lamenting, theorizing, and doing. Therefore, we must have a daily period when we stop our busyness and still the inner bedlam. But we must understand that the journey into absolute quietness of soul is not without danger; we may well hear other voices and think they are God.

This is particularly a danger if one perceives silence to be *emptiness.* To let one's mind go blank and open to the spiritual world without any direction or understanding of what one is doing gives access to evil as well as good.

This can be illustrated by a container in which a vacuum has been produced. When the stopper is removed, whatever is outside rushes in—not only fresh air, but polluted air as well. Even so, when the mind becomes a void or vacuum, and we open to the spiritual dimension, anything can jump in.

Totally emptying one's mind is the technique used in meditation to detach oneself from the world in order to merge with the Cosmic Mind. The meditator strives to reach a state of nothingness or impersonal consciousness. Transcendental Meditation (TM), which is nothing less than Hinduism dressed in acceptable Western garb, is practiced "to find the God within oneself." To reach the stage of God consciousness through TM, one must first go through a series of stages of cosmic consciousness and transcendental consciousness—whatever these are.

The "god within," for whom one supposedly searches through TM and other forms of Hinduism, is not the Supreme Being revealed in Holy Scriptures. He is not the heavenly Father which Jesus Christ came to reveal. Rather, the "god within" is described as Creative or Perfect Intelligence, Ultimate Being, or Ultimate Reality. The Lord God Jehovah, of course, is all of these—but He is so much more.

Asceticism within a "Christian" context also seeks mystical experience through total detachment from the physical self and outer world. Whatever the form of meditation, if one loses touch with the outer world, one can come under demonic influence.

The ultimate goal of Christian meditation is not to merge with the Divine. After all, we are not on the same level as God and never shall be. Nor is the ultimate goal to hear His voice or to receive guidance. The ultimate goal is *transformation.* In Christian meditation, we seek to know Him, to relate to Him, and to allow the Holy Spirit to transform us into the image of Christ that we might glorify Him.

Recently, I attended a retreat led by the Reverend Morton Kelsey, Episcopal priest, theologian, psychologist, prolific writer, and probably the foremost teacher today on the subject of Christian meditation. Because of the risks involved, he relentlessly warns against *imageless* prayer and meditation.

As I listened to him and read his books, I began to realize the part that imagery plays in my own personal prayer life. Before, I never gave it much thought. It just seemed natural to "practice the Presence of God"—Brother Lawrence's term for Christian meditation. I know of no better way to protect oneself from the intrusion of evil.

One means to inner quietness is to repeat Scripture, saying the verses slowly, trying to feel and picture what they mean. The picture a word evokes gives the word content. The name of a person causes us to visualize that person—his face, something about him, and perhaps his action in a certain situation. As I read or quote Scripture, my mind pictures the words to make them come alive for me.

In practicing His presence, I also find that softly praying in tongues, the language of the Spirit, is remarkably calming. Time and the push of doing, planning, or trying to figure out the weighty problems of life are suspended. I experience a oneness with the Spirit of God by letting my spirit flow with the mind of the Spirit in praise, worship, and intercession. Then, as I wait quietly in His presence, God often speaks—in a variety of ways.

Vizualizing Christ himself near me is another helpful means of making me more aware of Christ's immanence. Consciously relaxing my body, I visualize Jesus sitting in the large easy chair in our living room. I am at His feet, looking up into His face. We smile, but do not talk. Breathing slowly and deeply, I relax and allow His peace to permeate my mind and body. I am content simply to be near Him, secure in His love and presence—my Lord and Savior, Redeemer, and Friend.

Another imaginative experience I still employ first took place years ago, during a critical illness in the hospital. I was undergoing some tests which were frightening to one as sick as I was. As I lay on the X-ray table, I closed my eyes, held out my hand and whispered, "Jesus, please hold my hand." Since I knew He was with me, it was simple to imagine His taking my hand and holding it firmly in His. A few deep breaths exhaled slowly and I settled down, letting myself feel His hand clasping mine. To this day, I remember the heightened awareness of His presence and the serenity that it brought.

But, you wonder, since I consciously form these pictures, doesn't the ensuing quietness stem purely from my imagination? Not at all! Yes, the images are created by me. But the reality is Jesus' promise, "And surely I will be with you alway."[31] Through His Spirit, *He is with me.* And He is peace. As I reach out in the night, or at some dark moment, to whisper, "Jesus, hold my hand," I am affirming the promise of His presence. As I imagine my hand tucked in His and center my thinking on Jesus and His love for me, I actually open myself to Him.

Of course, all images and impressions which come to us through meditation must be checked with the Scriptures and what we know of God's ways in history. We dare not go dashing after fantasies of the mind which do not center in Jesus, the living Christ. Always Christian meditation and guidance is based on the premise that it is the crucified and risen Christ who leads us to God. Jesus said, plainly, "Unless you know me, you can't know the Father."[32] And, since it is Christ, the living Word, who reveals the Father, all revelation will be grounded in the written Word.

4. *Hearing and obedience.* When Jesus talked about guiding His own, He used the imagery of the shepherd and his flock. He emphasized the *mutual relationship* and *personal knowledge* between the shepherd and the sheep. His sheep follow the shepherd, He said, because they know the shepherd's voice. Then He spoke these marvelously reassuring words: "I am the good shepherd; I know my sheep and my sheep know me."[33]

If we are to become familiar with His voice, of course, we must *hear* God speak. But the word "to hear" in the Bible always carries the connotation of action—obedience to what we hear God say. So learning to know God's voice is clearly contingent on obedience.

5. *Discernment.* Because of Satan's uncanny ability to imitate, we need keen perception to differentiate between what is of God and what is not. Natural reasoning and intuition are not enough.

Spiritual discernment comes with spiritual maturity. To become mature, we must go beyond the elementary teachings about Christ and constantly feed on the solid meat of the

Word—the teaching about righteousness. In this way, the writer of Hebrews tells us, we train ourselves "to distinguish good from evil."[34]

We also need the spiritual discernment which comes as a *gift* of the Holy Spirit. God can and will supernaturally reveal evil which masks itself as good, so it is important that we pray for this gift.

Conclusion

Blind skiers swishing down a slope at exhilarating speeds are a spectacular, almost-unbelievable sight. Their amazing performance is possible, I am told, because they rely on the voice of their guide skiing directly ahead. Obviously, the blind person's flight downhill would be a catastrophe if he did not know the voice of his guide and follow it closely.

Not a one of us can negotiate the rugged and hazardous terrain of life safely on our own. Like the blind skier, we must follow hard on the heels of our Guide. Only as we maintain an intimate relationship with Christ, by spending time alone in communion with Him, by consistent obedience to the Word, and by the gift of the Holy Spirit, will we learn to know God's voice in whatever form He chooses to speak to us.

This is not only a vital requirement for Christian living, it can be a matter of life or death.

9

Thus Saith Who?

To avoid deception, it is crucial that we be able to spot the impostor who confronts us with the claim, "God told me . . ." First of all, we need to know why men and women misuse this loaded expression.

Justification for Selfishness

"God told me" is often a ploy to get one's own way. What we see is a person trying to justify some wrong behavior. If we want something badly enough, it is easy to convince ourselves that we are following God's orders—or at least that we have His okay. If God said do it, that makes any action legitimate. True!—*if* God said it. But if not, we will be self-deceived.

Take for example Peggy, who told me she was going to marry Peter. I knew Peter did not pretend to be a Christian. When she made her announcement, a scene that happened years before flashed to mind—a distraught wife spilling out the anguish and heartache of a wretched marriage. As an early teenager she went to church regularly. But then she married, and her husband had no time for God or the church. Since they lived in the country, and she didn't drive, she had no way to go to church and was cut off from Christian fellowship. What gripped me most were the bitter words, "No one ever told me it was wrong to marry a non-Christian." She'd paid for it, she said, living in hell these twenty years.

142

Peggy wasn't going to be able to say, "No one told me." "How can you?" I challenged her. "Don't you know the Bible expressly forbids a believer to be yoked together with an unbeliever?"[1]

She shrugged. "My mother was a Christian when she married my father. He wasn't and isn't a Christian, but they're happy." Since she and Peter were "so much in love," and "so right for each other," she argued, God must have brought them together. Nothing I could say would dissuade her. But there was no doubt that what Peggy claimed God wanted for her was in reality her own "I want!"

Peggy's self-deception began when she started dating an unbeliever. Regarding such relationships, the Bible asks: "For what do righteousness and wickedness have in common? Or what fellowship can light have with darkness?. . . What does a believer have in common with an unbeliever? What agreement is there between the temple of God and idols?"[2]

The answer is plain. In things that really matter, we have *nothing* in common. Surely, then, a man or woman who finds so much in common with an unbeliever that he or she can even consider marriage needs to face the question honestly: How come? Is the attraction primarily physical? Have my priorities and goals shifted to those of the world? Am I kicking the lordship of Christ?

Attempting to justify the relationship, Peggy contended that since Peter believed in God, he could not be regarded as an "unbeliever."

But this sort of thinking is grounded in deception. The word "believer" (Greek, *pistos*) means "to entrust oneself to." Biblically, a believer is one who has entrusted himself to Christ, has become one with Him, and who lives in obedience to His words. This is what distinguishes a believer from an unbeliever, and, accordingly, settles with whom we may or may not link our lives.

Another way Peggy made herself vulnerable to self-deception was when she determined that "being happy" was more important than being obedient. Pursuing misplaced priorities can easily lead to deception.

I'm well aware that some Christians do violate God's clear command; they date, marry, and enter business partnerships with non-Christians—and seemingly get away with it. Others even use this fact to justify doing the same thing. Those of us looking on find ourselves wrestling the age-old question: Why does God tolerate such disobedience, even seemingly blessing the disobedient ones?

The prophet Habakkuk took both the question and his complaint directly to God. The answer he received was to wait patiently for God to manifest His justice. So must you and I. In the meantime, God expects personal faith and obedience.

If those who violate God's commands seem happy, successful, and blessed by God, so what? *Biblical principles do not stand or fall on the basis of who is doing what and seemingly getting away with it.*

Since God is not going to say anything contradictory to His written Word, we have to conclude that Peggy's claim that God okayed her marriage to Peter was either a lie or self-deception.

God is not capricious. His commands are lovingly given for our protection. Because God is a God of undeviating righteousness, there are no loopholes. Marrying an unbeliever or doing anything else that God so plainly forbids is flagrant disobedience. No matter that we claim God's approval; if we turn our back on God's protective principles, we are subject to Satan's tyranny.

A Tool to Manipulate Others

Some instances of "God told me" seem to spring from the subconscious need to punish oneself or play the martyr's role. This *may* be the reason behind a protracted fast. The need for self-punishment or self-martyrdom can also express itself in hair, shirts, shaved heads, or some ugly form of dress. Yet the rationale is, "God said . . ." I've even known individuals, carrying a tremendous load of guilt over past sexual sins, to claim "God told me" no more making love with their marriage partner—in direct opposition to the Scriptures (e.g., 1 Cor. 7:4, 5).

Behind some other cases of "God told me" is the subconscious desire to come across as a super-saint. The emphasis is not on *what* God said, but that He spoke to *me*. What He is supposed to have said may even be in accordance with the Scriptures. Still, the words are a delusion arising from the desire to impress others.

"God told me" can also be a tool to manipulate those who oppose us. A leader may exert control over a group by claiming that he alone has the word of God in a given situation. A father may use "God told me" to control his family according to his own selfish whims. A wife may say "God told me" to get her own way, or to override her husband's decision. A person may pressure others in a group situation, saying, "God told me," in order to push through some personal choice. Unless what the person declares is in violation of the Scriptures, refuting him is difficult.

Back when our three boys were little, a woman phoned to ask me to baby-sit—for free. The reason? She and her husband sang in various churches, and taking along their son who was severely crippled was difficult. Her point was that I should do it because Jerry, an adopted child, was "special" to the Lord. Special, she said, because Satan stamped him at birth, crippling him. (A strange idea, I thought.) By taking care of Jerry, I'd be doing something special for God.

As it was, my physical problems made caring for my own youngsters almost more than I could handle. And Jerry, a heavy boy, required lots of lifting, something I definitely was not to do. Her way of asking let me know that she would view a refusal as my saying no to God. I was grateful when my husband rescued me by putting his foot down.

This same woman used the "God told me" approach on a mutual friend who pastored a tiny congregation. Somehow, somebody had helped him to get a new automobile. A short time later this woman came to him with "a word from the Lord" that he should give her and her husband the car for their "ministry." Fortunately, the pastor was not intimidated by her.

One afternoon Al and I were listening on the radio to a preacher who was drawing enormous crowds in his tent crusades. Claiming a "miracle ministry," he described how even at that moment the oil of the Holy Spirit was pouring from his hands. He claimed, too, that oil flowed from the hands of those for whom he prayed. For a donation, one could get a "healing cloth" with some of this oil wiped on it. "The Word says!" he shrieked, " 'Give to every man that asketh of thee; and of him that taketh away thy goods ask them not again.'[3] Now I'm asking you to send me your gold rings, your jewelry, your watches, and your money. If you don't, you are disobeying God!"

He was employing Satan's age-old trick of quoting the Scriptures perversely—a trick used by many false prophets. How many unwary sheep were thus fleeced only God knows. Whether or not this big-name preacher was a "miracle worker," I could not say. I suspected he was one of the "many" Jesus said would claim miracles as a credential for getting into heaven, but whom Jesus would disclaim ever knowing. Unless he repented of the deception he practiced, it seemed inevitable that his end would be tragic. And it was. Furthermore, the circumstances of his death were an unfortunate reproach to the gospel of Christ.

False Prophets Examined

It is no light thing to say "God told me" or "God said" in order to serve one's own end. The Old Testament recounts the tragic aftermath when a nation's prophets claimed "God said" when God had not spoken. Six centuries before Christ, thousands in Judah were taken captive and carried away to Babylon. Yet those Israelites still in Jerusalem lived under the delusion that in spite of their gross sins, God would not destroy them. The weeping and warnings of Jeremiah failed to move them to repentance. Their security, they asserted, was in the temple. Surely God would preserve the temple where He had put His name.

Ezekiel knew better. As God's messenger, he strove to bring both his fellow-exiles and those at Jerusalem to their senses. He laid bare the sins of the nation, pronouncing God's impending judgment. At the same time he denounced the officials and priests who practiced extortion and coercion to rip off the people, he indicted the prophets. His charge? They were telling the people, " 'This is what the Sovereign Lord says'—when the Lord has not spoken." The penalty? God said, "I will pour out my wrath on them and consume them with my fiery anger."[4]

The menace of lying prophets was also a weighty concern of the New Testament writers. False prophets, Peter cautions, will "exploit you with stories they have made up."[5] Since the Greek word *emporos*, translated "exploit," has commercial connotations, Peter seems to have in mind particularly those who prophesy lies to reap financial gain. He then recounts the historic record of men and angels who rejected God's authority and ran head-on into terrible judgment. Consider what happened to these individuals, he warns. Know that this is the certain destiny of all whose interest is self-indulgence. Don't think anyone who claims "God said," when the words are his own, will escape. Destruction "waits for them with unsleeping eyes."[6]

As Christians, we tend to think that whenever God promises something good, He is talking to us personally, but whenever He promises judgment, He is talking about someone else. We are apt to shrug off the condemnation of false prophets as having nothing to do with us. But anyone who declares "Thus saith the Lord . . ." when God has not spoken is a false prophet who will come under God's judgment.

Examples Where Prophecy Is Misused

The charismatic renewal has seen a resurgence of those gifts of the Spirit which Paul lists as being for the "common good." The gift of prophecy is manifested when an individual speaks forth a message which does not originate in the intellect. It is directed from God through our spirit to our mind. It is the "God said" gift, which, Paul said, may serve to convince an unbeliever that he is a sinner and bring him to Christ. The primary purpose of this gift though is to *strengthen, encourage, and comfort* fellow believers.[7]

What has happened is that many have recast the gift of prophetic utterance into something that could well be dubbed "charismatic fortune-telling."

God has promised us guidance. We can count on it. At the same time, He has forbidden us to pry into the future. But many try to sneak around God's off-limits sign by way of prophetic gifts. Among some groups, it is common practice for persons seeking guidance to corner one another to "get a personal word from the Lord." Members promiscuously prophesy over each other, and whatever is spoken is taken as from God. Unhappily, deception is often the bitter result.

I've seen it happen far too often. Individuals who thought they were hearing a message from God, finding out later they accepted a lie of the devil. By that time they are reduced to a shambled heap.

Because of the emotional factors involved, probably no personal prophecy has created more human wreckage than the matchmaking directives. "Thus saith the Lord: John is to marry Susie . . ."

This is exactly what happened to a friend of ours. She and the man she dated attended a fellowship group together. From time to time, different individuals prophesied that they were to marry, but years passed and there was no wedding. Obviously, the man was simply using her (and more so because of the prophecy!), while she clung desperately to "what God said." The emotional upheaval finally brought her very near to suicide, and she has been years recovering from the trauma.

What about those who prophesied the two would marry? How do they explain the prophecy not being fulfilled? They say that they spoke God's will, but the man simply refused to obey. But the Bible says that if what a prophet says does not come to pass, the message is not of the Lord. Rather, the prophet has spoken presumptuously.[8]

Don't assume though that just because a prophecy is fulfilled, it has to be from God; God may have had nothing to do with it. For instance, a girl told me how she and her husband came to be married. She hadn't liked him at all at first, she said. Then they received a prophecy that they were to marry. They married, and now she loved him dearly. When I was in that area for meetings a couple of years later, the same girl came up and greeted me. When I asked how she was doing, she beamed, "Oh, I'm divorced now. Praise the Lord!" *The result of another prophecy?* I wondered.

Another case in point. When I heard Tom and Barb Pringle tell how God had said they should come together with Doug Dwyer and Grace Cook in communal living and start a ministry, I had serious doubts. They were relatively new Christians and the Bible states that immature Christians are not to hold leadership positions—for their protection as well as the protection of the flock.

As their story unfolded, I was further alerted by the heavy

attention given to demons, by much of self in what they claimed God was saying, and by their separatist attitude. Relating how they left their church when prophecy came through Barb to leave NOW, Tom elaborated, "His Church cannot function within the bounds of the denomination."

I not only knew better, but Tom's statement brought back vivid memories of the Jesus People. Girls and boys who had been heavy into the drug scene only weeks before said the same thing. On streetcorners, in parks, from makeshift platforms, they waved their Bibles and proclaimed the churches were the "Jezebel" of Revelation. A large part of the Jesus People wanted no part of the established Church.

Many of these young people started out well, but in their sweeping rejection of the Church, they forfeited all the teaching and wisdom of the Early Church fathers who knew God in a very real way. They cut themselves off from the experienced leadership, the structured discipline, and the sound Bible teaching— not found in some churches, granted, but certainly found in others—which they desperately needed for sound spiritual growth. Consequently, the casualty rate was enormous.

This is not to say that God will never lead people out of their church. He does. But the fact that certain denominations have restricted the work of the Holy Spirit within their domain is no reason to write off all organized churches. Suppose every Spirit-filled man and woman walked out of the denominational churches. What then? This would not release them from the biblical injunction to meet regularly together. The upshot would be a host of new denominations—no matter what those who left called themselves.

The Pringles also claimed that God continually led them step by step in minute detail—by directive personal prophecy. But these prophetic utterances *all came between each other*. In other words, Tom prophesied what he himself or Doug or Barb or Grace should do, and they in turn gave directive prophecies to the others in this inner-directed group. Is that how the Bible says it should be? No, prophecies are to be spoken before the church, and others are to judge. These are imperative safeguards.

When a handful of close-knit people prophesy over each other with guidance, personal "I wants" or "I thinks" unconsciously seep into the message. There is no one present to judge objectively. And because the group is inner-directed, the individuals are likely to reinforce each other in the delusion that this is God.

In the case of the Pringles, the delusion was clearly seen when they said that God showed them Doug was to divorce his wife and marry Grace. Tom even claimed he prophetically performed the marriage ceremony!

Continuing to be directed by prophecy, they acquired land and began building, envisioning a community where God could bring His Body together. Over the months, a smattering of others joined the project. Now Tom was saying that God had shown them they were to go to South America. Doug was taking flying lessons in view of locating a jungle hideaway where the group could settle "to escape the judgment coming to the United States." This situation would also prepare them for what they were to do "after the tribulation."

The South America venture was short-lived—Doug was killed when his plane crashed; the others are back in the States; the "community" has fallen apart.

Were the Pringles mistaken in the voice they followed? They say no. Asked about the discrepancy between what God allegedly spoke to them in prophecy and the written Word, they become extremely defensive. Directive prophecy of a leading nature, they admit, plays a tremendous part in their lives, and will continue to do so. Barb contends that deception was impossible since she did not give Satan any authority to dictate to her, but gave it wholly to God.

The fact is that we do not have to give Satan permission to dictate in order to be misled. We get into trouble the minute we accept as valid a message which goes directly against the Scriptures. Such is any message which has God shuffling marriage partners to create more-spiritual unions.

Even though the Bible expressly forbids dissolution of the marriage union, Satan has had appalling success in selling the lie that it is not only right but expedient to break up a marriage in-order for one partner to marry a more spiritual person. If this were true, no Christian marriage would be secure. Marriage vows would neither be sacred nor binding, but subject to the whims of the "more spiritual."

The Apostle Paul does say, "If the unbeliever leaves, let him do so. A believing man or woman is not bound in such circumstances."[9] But this pronouncement comes on the heels of his emphatic injunction that no man may divorce his wife on the grounds that she is an unbeliever, let alone because she hasn't attained the same spiritual rank. He applies the same rule to the wife. Prophecy to the contrary can only be a lie of Satan—not an oracle of God.

A Personal Encounter

My first encounter with personal prophecy occurred during a period when I was in and out of the hospital with frequent hemorrhages. I was sitting in a testimony meeting when a woman suddenly jumped to her feet. Her shrill, rapid-fire words were leveled directly at me. The gist of them was that God had just healed me.

In an instant, everyone stood up praising God. Everyone, that is, except me. I was too shocked to do anything but sit numbly and wonder at what was going on. I certainly had no witness in my spirit that God was speaking to me. Instead, the message left me cold, partly because I did not believe God would pick such a messenger. I knew the woman had been involved in an affair and that she was at that time living in adultery. Once she had told me laughingly, "—but the Lord blesses us in spite of what we do."

God may choose as His mouthpiece someone frail and weak. But morally corrupt? No! God said concerning the lying prophets of Jerusalem, "I have seen something horrible: They commit adultery and live a lie. . . . Do not listen to [them]. . . ."[10]

Accordingly, I believe that God doesn't want me to give assent to those "who wag their own tongues,"[11] but claim to be the oracle of God. The evil that God rejects I am also to reject.

I remember the chill in my spirit when a stranger jumped up in our church in the middle of a service, ranting that an unclean spirit was present—"thus saith the Lord."

The pastor quietly informed the congregation that neither he nor his elders knew this man. And, "We do not accept prophecy from anyone we do not know."

The man rushed down the aisle, spewing out warnings that he had better accept it. In the meantime, the elders moved to the back of the church. Obviously, the man needed help, but before they could get him into the foyer, the stranger struck out, ripping the shirt of one elder.

After talking with the man in private, the pastors agreed there certainly were unclean spirits in the service—the source, this self-appointed prophet. They offered help, but he refused.

The Ultimate Offense

Verbally forging God's name to their own religious babbling is precisely what the false prophets did when they prophesied peace to Jerusalem when there was no peace.[12] Brazenly, they declared, "The Lord said," when the Lord said no such thing. In fact, God was saying just the opposite of peace. It was the hour of judgment. Multiplied warnings had failed to turn Israel and Judah back to God. And now Jeremiah prophesied impending doom: captivity, torture, and death at the hands of the Babylonians.

Actually, Israel's false prophets were simply mouthing Satan's Big Lie: *You can sin and get away with it.* Thumbing their noses at Jeremiah's forecast of exile to Babylon, they filled the people with false hope. Assuring "all who follow the stubbornness of their hearts . . . no harm will come to you."[13]

Moreover, because God is scrupulous in keeping His word, they had the audacity to expect Him to fulfill their lying prophecies. What else could He do? they reasoned. Surely He would have to save His reputation. When the prophecies did not come to pass, men and women who believed the reckless lies would bitterly claim Yahweh failed to honor His word. If God didn't do as they prophesied, the whole idea of "the word of the Lord" would be brought into disrepute.

The false prophets did not back God into a corner, but their attempt pushed Israel over the line to where repentance was no longer possible. Indeed, Jeremiah was told not to pray any longer for the well-being of this people. God was outraged. "I will allow no pity or mercy or compassion to keep me from destroying them," He said.[14]

What a sobering thought! God did not only condemn the licentious priests and lying prophets to judgment; *those who listened to their lies* would likewise "perish by the sword and famine."[15]

And what of the hour in which we live? Christians who may or may not claim spiritual gifts, babble the same false message of peace. God's punishment pronounced for shameless, brazen sin is pooh-poohed. And the deceived propagate—and live by—the twisted message of God's "unconditional love." Though mouthed in various ways, "You can sin and get away with it" is still the Big Lie.

The theme of the best-attended meetings I have ever seen in a college setting was this: "It doesn't matter what you have done, God isn't mad at you." Put another way, "You can't do anything bad enough to escape God's love. He loves you—regardless."

I suspect that Paul would have shot from his seat with a scorching rebuke had he been there. Paul took a tough view of such corrupted teaching. Sexual immorality, impurity, and greed, he wrote to the believers at Ephesus, are "improper for God's holy people." He warned, "Let no one deceive you with empty words, for because of such things God's wrath comes on those who are disobedient."[16] Yes, God's *wrath*!

It is one thing to say to a sinner, "No matter what sins you have committed in the past, God still loves you. And if you are truly sorry and willing to forsake your sin, God will accept you just as you are, forgive you, and cleanse you from all unrighteousness."[17] But it is quite another to say to Christians that God's unconditional love means He is indifferent to obdurate disobedience. This, Paul says, is nothing less than "empty words" to deceive.

I'll never forget my consternation at what a fellow church member once said to me. Though I knew none of the details, I was aware that her husband had been married before. That day, as we rocked our babies in the church nursery, she spoke about her husband's divorce and their subsequent marriage. "We knew when we got married it was wrong," she said, with a little smile and a shrug. "But we also knew God would forgive us."

That same sort of twisted thinking was recently expressed by another young mother, one I've watched with anguish as she disregarded her marriage vows and broke up the family to marry another. "I know divorce is wrong—but God is bigger than divorce."

I thought, He sure is! To be a victim of divorce is one thing. But to walk straight into adultery, shrugging off the sin as inconsequential—asserting God's "unconditional love"—is irrational. Sin invariably has its consequences.

Isaiah 40:12-31 is a superb and electrifying poem on the incomparable greatness of God. But you don't understand, says the prophet, if you think the transcendency of God means He is too great to care; our heartaches, our hardships, and our helplessness do not go unnoticed by Him. But, then, neither do our sins. Those who smirk that God cannot see or know what evil they do in the darkness will be destroyed by a God from whom no one can hide.[18]

After Moses' death, God commissioned Joshua to lead His people into the Promised Land. To allay Joshua's fears, He promised, "I will never leave you nor forsake you. . . ."[19]

Two miracles followed: the people crossed the Jordan River on dry ground, and Jericho's walls collapsed at a shout. But only days later, God thundered, "I will NOT be with you anymore unless you destroy whatever among you is devoted to destruction."[20] (Emphasis mine.)

What stirred God to such severity? Achan's sin.

Jericho was a stupendous victory for Israel. But stickey-fingered Achan sneaked home with a beautiful Babylonian robe, 200 shekels of silver, and a wedge of gold. He buried the loot under his tent floor, thinking no one would be the wiser. But the very next time the army faced the enemy at Ai, something happened which had never happened before: Israelite blood was spilled in battle.

Joshua was frantic; where was Yahweh now? Tearing his clothes and throwing himself on the ground, he beseeched God: What about God's covenant of love? What of His promise never to leave or forsake His people? Didn't Yahweh know His name was at stake? What would the heathen say about Israel's God now?

"Stand up! Joshua. And stop worrying about My name," God

ordered. "You'd better start searching the camp."[21]

God had not violated His covenant of love, but His covenant was with "those who love him and keep his commands."[22] Achan's sin had made the Israelites "liable to destruction." Because of His very nature, God simply could not bless Israel until that sin was dealt with.

That believers should presume on God's love was a painful worry to Peter. False prophets had shown up in the New Testament church, and the Apostle warned, "They will tell you it doesn't make any difference what you do. But don't believe them." As for those who spread such lies, he had a sobering word: "If they have escaped the corruption of the world by knowing our Lord and Savior Jesus Christ and are again entangled in it and overcome, they are worse off at the end than they were at the beginning. It would have been better for them not to have known the way of righteousness, than to have known it and then to turn their backs on the sacred commandment. . . ."[23]

Yet Christians glibly quote, "If we are faithless, he will remain faithful." The inference is that even when we go our own way and do what we please, God is still faithful to bless us. But that is hardly what this verse is saying.

We need to look at what goes before and after. Notice, "If we disown him [and we do when we turn to our own way], he will also disown us; if we are faithless, he will remain faithful, for he cannot disown himself."[24]

Now when God says, "He cannot disown himself," He is *not* saying our faithlessness doesn't matter, that He will bless us anyway. He is saying that whatever we do, He can only respond according to who He is—"the Lord who exercises kindness, justice and righteousness on earth, for in these I delight."[25] God cannot deny His lovingkindness. But neither can He deny His righteous judgment for sin. "To be false to Himself is something which even omnipotent God cannot be," says one Bible commentator.[26]

To be sure, God's love and mercy and grace endure forever.[27] They reach to the depths of man's depravity to recreate and restore whenever there is true repentance. But it is an affront to God to deliberately do what God condemns and then take refuge in His amazing love and grace.

Moreover, the Scriptures are very clear, any message which denies or evades the truth of God's judgment for sin is rooted in deception. God's love *does* endure forever—but so does His righteous judgment.

The True Gift

Because so many human voices claim to be messengers of God, spiritual discernment is imperative. On the one hand, believing a false prophecy can have tragic consequences. On the other, prophecy which is truly of God can bring tremendous blessing. As to the efficacy of true prophecy, let me relate two examples from my own experience.

In the first instance, I was going through bleak weeks of depression and despair, feeling alienated from family, from friends, and from God. The turning point came (as I described in *Lord of the Valleys*)[28] when God showed me something about His love I had not seen before. It was this: Lazarus was not delivered from death because of his love for Jesus. Rather, it was Christ's *perfect* love for Lazarus which set him free. Like a crack of light in the stifling darkness, I saw that I could never love enough to free me from the fears which tormented me. If I were set free, it would be because God's "perfect love casts out [or, drives out] all fear."[29]

The next Sunday night everyone had left the church sanctuary except my husband, myself, and our beloved friend and pastor. He spoke quietly, but with authority: "You don't have to go on another day tormented by fear."

As I knelt at the altar, he laid his hands on my head and began to speak God's words: "Daughter, I have called you and made you Mine. . . . My love casts out all fear. . . ." The words were spoken softly, but they were charged with the healing power of God. At that moment, I felt a mighty onrush of God's love. It flowed through the top of my head, surging through my body, forcing out all fear.

He went on speaking as the Spirit prompted. "I call My own sheep by name. I lead them out. I go before them, and My sheep follow Me. *Know that you aren't going any place I haven't been before!*"

My tears were no longer tears of despair; they were tears of relief. God was my heavenly Father; I did belong to Him; His love had carved this valley—the devil was a liar! As God's love flowed into my body, mind, and spirit, the dark fears left. Praise the Lord! I was free—gloriously free!

I cannot recall all the words of prophecy spoken that night, but I do know that God indicated that the tenth chapter of John would mean much to me; in the present situation, and again, in a future crisis. When I got up from the altar rail, I knew by experience that when God's perfect love comes in, fear has to go!

The tenth chapter of John had long been familiar but as I read through it the next day, God stopped me at the twenty-ninth verse: "No man is able to pluck them out of my Father's hand." What I heard was: *Stop blaming others for your spiritual smashups.*

It had been easy to blame my husband; if only he was more spiritual, more loving, more understanding, I could be a better Christian. And I blamed others, feeling their un-Christlike attitudes and actions had augmented my depression. But even if this was the case, Jesus was emphatic: No one—not my husband nor any other person—could snatch me out of His hand. Blaming others for my estrangement from God was self-deception.

This does not mean we are unaffected by the quality of spiritual life around us. We are, very much so. This is why Paul wrote, "Encourage one another and build each other up."[30] And why Jesus warned against being a stumbling block, an offense to our brothers and sisters in Christ.[31]

But the Bible also says, "Build *yourselves* up in your most holy faith, and pray in the Holy Spirit. Keep *yourselves* in God's love."[32] (Emphasis mine.) And this is what God was saying to me.

It was the gift of prophecy which God used to release me from fear, and to minister in a very personal way—strength, encouragement, comfort.

The other incident took place a few years later under quite different circumstances. It was a summer camp meeting at Elim Bible Institute. Friday was given to fasting and prayer in the tabernacle, and to special ministry by the leadership. As missionaries, pastors, and their wives, in turn, sat in two chairs placed down front, there was the laying on of hands with prayer for the presenting need. Often there was prophecy.

On this particular occasion, I was asked to join in praying for a missionary wife, broken in health. After we had prayed for her, President Carlton Spencer pointed at me. "Sit down, we're going to pray for you." I gulped—and sat. I knew he was aware of problems and pressures, but this was totally unexpected.

Carlton prayed. Silence. Just as I wondered if I should get up, the only minister in the group whose name I did not know began to speak. "I don't know this woman," he explained, "so I didn't know whether or not to say this. But as we prayed, I saw a high board fence . . . a *very high* board fence. It wasn't held together by wooden stringers, but by steel bands. This woman was going around and around inside the fence looking for a way out. Suddenly, a hand reached down with a large pair of tin snips and cut those steel bands. The boards fell outward and she went thataway!" His hand cut a swift path through the air.

I looked at Carlton and started to laugh. "I know every board, every knothole in that fence!" I said, "Remember? One of the chapters in the *Lord of the Valleys* is 'Who Builds the Fences?' "

It was true. Once again I was looking for a way over, a way under, a way to slip through the fence that hedged me in. And God used prophecy to make me realize what I was up to. I got the message loud and clear: Stop trying to find your own way out of your problems! Remember who builds the fences. . . . God can and will remove them in His time.

A Review of the Guidelines

I don't question the value or validity of personal prophecy—when it is of God. But when it comes to any message—personal or public—which claims "God said," we need to look at it from two perspectives: the message and the messenger.

The Message

1. If he foretells something, does it come to pass? (Deut. 18:22; Jer. 28:9).
2. Coming to pass is not enough: What is the spiritual quality of the message? Does it point one to God? (Deut. 13:1-5).

3. Does his message or teaching harmonize 100 percent with the Word of God? Does it weaken the authority of God's Word? Does it distort Scripture? Does it add to the Scriptures? Does it lay aside Scripture and claim that this is a new revelation of God? (Prov. 30:5, 6; Isa. 8:20; Rom. 15:4; 2 Tim. 3:16; Rev. 19:10).

4. Does the prophecy lean toward building God's kingdom or man's kingdom? (2 Cor. 4:5).

5. Does the message cater to our pride or propose self-gratification? (1 John 2:16).

6. Does the message contain an element of hope—or is it completely condemning? (John 14:16; Rev. 12:10).

The Messenger

1. What is the messenger's moral character? Does he live a life of holiness? Of openness and honesty? (Isa. 28:7; Jer. 23:11, 14; 6:13).

2. What is the messenger's attitude toward personal status and success? Toward money? (Jer. 6:13; Mic. 3:11; 1 Tim. 6:5; Titus 1:10, 11).

3. Is the messenger caught up with his own importance? Is his first commitment to pleasing God—or pleasing people? (Acts 20:19; 1 Thess. 2:3, 4).

4. Does he use his power unjustly? Does he manipulate people to his own end? (Jer. 23:10; Jude 12, 16).

5. Does he consider that he has the last word, or is he willing to submit the message to others to be judged? (1 Cor. 14:29).

6. Does his life demonstrate emotional and spiritual stability? (2 Pet. 2:17; Jude 12).

Other Factors to Watch For

1. *Beware of those who come to you at a low point in your life.*

   Be particularly cautious of the person who says, "No one cares about you but me. . . . Your parents don't care or understand. . . . Your husband (or wife) doesn't care or understand like I do. . . ."

   If your marriage is in trouble, beware of the person who says, "I've been through divorce. I understand and will stick by you. . . ," and then encourages you to confide in him or her.

2. *Prophecy which does not flow through the screen of love will come out polluted, since we tend to project our prejudices and inner malignancies.*

   Paul, instructing the church as to the proper use of the gifts, emphasizes the importance of love. In contrast to those who teach by cunning and craftiness and deceitful scheming, he charges us to speak the truth in love (1 Cor. 14:1; Eph. 4:15).

3. *If the message is from God, we do not have to manipulate people or try to manipulate God to bring it to pass.*

   Remember, it was after Samuel secretly anointed David to be king that David slew Goliath and became one of Saul's armor-bearers. But shortly, Saul saw David as his enemy to be destroyed. Forced to flee for his life, David found himself time and again in a position to have killed Saul, and he could have honestly claimed self-defense. What's more, he might have reasoned that since he was already anointed by God to be king, he would be putting into effect God's will, as spoken by Samuel.

   When it comes to prophecy, God's timing is as important as God's call.

4. *Check out the prophet's background if he suddenly appears as a loner with no credentials. A loner often turns out to be a lone wolf in sheep's clothing.*

   Personality and polish are too often misconstrued as spiritual power and authority.

5. *Don't ignore the response of your spirit.*

   We may hear a message that leaves us chilled, or we may feel nothing. Pray for discernment. God wants to sharpen our spiritual perception.

6. *As a general rule, prophecy (or tongues) will never interrupt the preaching or teaching of the Word.*

   If there should be an exception, it is only reasonable that the Holy Spirit would first impress the person teaching; the interruption would not come as a surprise to him. Otherwise, this sort of interruption is discourteous and causes confusion—something God does not author.

7. *If you receive a "word from the Lord" from someone privately,
   expose it to spiritually responsible persons.*

    Instantly reject the message which the messenger has told
you to keep secret. We do not have an option; "Others should
weigh carefully what is said" (1 Cor. 14:29). The gift of "the
ability to distinguish between spirits" should function here.
But neither should one ignore common sense. Paul once said,
"I speak to sensible people; judge for yourselves what I say"
(1 Cor. 10:15).

10

How a Good Church Can Go Bad

So many denominations and local assemblies are throwing their doors wide open to the grossest forms of deception, we might think the image of deception "creeping" into the Church hardly applies nowadays. But it does. Even churches that guard their gates from the more flagrant deceptions are finding Satan slipping in with his more foxy tricks.

We shouldn't be surprised that the churches most effectual in kingdom building are Satan's choicest targets. After all, Satan is irrevocably committed to bringing down God's kingdom. The Enemy knows that in order to destroy God's kingdom, he must destroy the local church.

Naturally, then, he zeroes in on those churches that are the most spiritually flourishing. And what better way for Satan to establish a beachhead than to deceive those responsible for making the decisions of the church? I was involved in just such a church.

First Church had not only wonderously affected my life, but it had a far-reaching effect on many lives. No gimmicks, just the presence and power of the Holy Spirit as Pastor Torrey faithfully preached the Word of God, his messages centering on prayer, holiness, the deeper life. The spiritual climate was so refreshing that a group of servicemen drove over one hundred miles to attend the services—even the midweek prayer meeting.

The elders were mature men of God, not the kind to be easily taken in by the devil's wiles. They knew the discipline of prayer and fasting in seeking God's will. Furthermore, this church was a missionary church, its emphasis on missions reflected by an exceptionally large missionary budget. Giving, however, didn't take the place of personal involvement; young people and adults together ministered in trailer parks, cotton camps, at street meetings, and at the skid-row mission.

In spite of these spiritual strengths for which First Church was renowned, there was an Enemy takeover.

How did Satan pull it off? It was hard to understand how men and women who apparently wanted God's will were duped into making a decision which proved fatal to the church. I felt that the example of First Church carried a warning, not only for local churches, but for any fellowship group or company of believers. Exposing the Enemy's methods in this instance should target danger areas for others in group decision-making. So I turned to Eric Kuhn, the one man who could give me some answers and needed insight.

For about seven years, Eric Kuhn was the elder responsible for the outreach ministry of First Church. During this time, the Lord also led him into an intercessory prayer ministry for the church. He would spend Saturday night from 11:00 p.m. till 4:00 a.m. Sundays at the church in prayer. He was to pray for Pastor Torrey, who carried on his ministry in spite of great physical suffering. And he was to pray for all pastors who were true ministers of God that the Word of God would go forth with power. Though these nights of prayer were often charged with the glory of God's presence, there were nights when he became engaged in open combat with the Enemy.

For four years Eric Kuhn faithfully kept his prayer vigil alone. Then two and sometimes three other men joined him. He said, "What a burden was lifted from my heart! And what power there was!" Soon there were two prayer groups. And the impact of those nights of intercession lasting over twelve years was clearly evidenced by the spiritual growth and vitality of the church.

From the beginning of his pastorate, Pastor Torrey was a sick man. But now he became bedfast. I wondered to what extent the gates of deception were opened by the manner in which Pastor Torrey's illness was handled. The true nature of his illness was never spoken of. Why, I am not sure. The fact was that he was terminally ill with TB. Those of us who knew, it seemed, were not supposed to know.

Perhaps the reason for the hush-hush was concern that some would protest—and prudently so—children and the feeble being exposed to an infectious disease. Perhaps the acknowledgment that his tuberculosis was active would have been seen as a lack of faith. For whatever reason, we went along with denying reality, playing our expected role well. Only on occasion, and only among close friends, did any of us admit we were not comfortable with the cover-up.

When Pastor Torrey could no longer leave his bed, Eric Kuhn's son, Kurt, who was the assistant pastor, and Ted Lytle, lay minister, filled the pulpit. Since Ted Lytle was older and more experienced, Pastor Torrey conferred on him the responsibility for leadership, though Pastor Torrey retained command. But by no means could a man so ill carry on efficiently. To spare him, the church members usually shielded him from critical problems in the church, but sometimes they gave him a distorted view. Satan exploited the situation, and by the time the decision was made to look for a new pastor, the church was in a miserable state.

Eventually, the official board located three prospective pastors. The church prayed that there would be no question; when we heard the man of God's choice, *we would know at that very time* that he was the one.

The first man was easily ruled out. The second came, and what a service! Never will I forget the marvelous presence of God as the Word was preached. The anointing of the Spirit was strikingly upon both the man and the message. Afterward, folks beamed and pumped one another's hand and said how Robert Briggs was surely God's appointed man, and what a wonderful answer to prayer.

Later, someone said we should hear the third candidate—just to be sure. And others shrugged, why not?

Someone could have pointed out that it was no little thing to disregard their prior witness that Robert Briggs was God's choice, that such rashness could lead to deception. But nobody did. So Paul Sparkman preached a trial sermon the following Sunday.

I knew nothing of the behind-the-scenes campaigning going on until the secretary of the church board called, polling to know which candidate the congregation favored. There was no question as to our choice. Robert Briggs was an answer to our prayers, didn't she agree?

Well, no . . . She thought Brother Sparkman with his academic degrees and intellectual approach might be more influential with the young people. She'd overheard a university student bait him with some hard questions, and the young man seemed impressed by the pastor's answers.

"But it's not as though Robert Briggs lacks education or intelligence," I protested.

But she rushed on, "Besides, since we've had the other kind [which I took to mean 'spiritual'], a change might be good. . . ."

I was stunned, and then I heard myself saying, "While you've been talking, the words keep coming to me, 'You shall eat of the book, and it shall be sweet in your mouth, but bitter in your belly.' "

I knew that similar words found in Ezekiel and Revelation meant something quite different, within their scriptural context, so I explained. "God seems to be saying that 'eating of the book,' in this case, symbolizes the choosing of a pastor on the basis of intellectualism and academic achievement over and above a man of great spiritual depth. No matter how 'sweet' the choice seems now, in the end, it will be a bitter one."

"What's that all about?" Al asked as I hung up the phone.

I shook my head. "You're not going to believe this . . ."

All week I tried to push aside feelings of apprehension by telling myself that men like Eric Kuhn could not miss God's guidance. God wouldn't let them. Nevertheless, in the end, the board voted unanimously to call Paul Sparkman as pastor, and he readily accepted.

I was baffled. Had the board made the wrong decision, or had I mistaken God's choice?

When the board called an unexpected church meeting the

following Saturday night, I wasn't sure I wanted to go. I figured what's done is done; nothing would be gained. But then again, Al and I would like some answers.

I appreciated the candor with which each one spelled out what swayed his or her vote. A number of board members said they had each come to their final decision after asking God—separately—for a "sign." Two members, for example, sought the opinion of teenagers. This disclosure, along with other dubious means of ascertaining God's will, only made us the more apprehensive. What alarmed me most was to hear it said that the church needed a change from the emphasis on "the victorious life" we'd known under Pastor Torrey. The devil, I thought, was surely doing cartwheels for sheer joy.

Soon after the board meeting, I awoke one morning right out of a vivid dream—sobbing. This was what I dreamed:

My husband and I were part of a small informal meeting in a side room at the church. We sat in a half-circle, praying and sharing together with a dozen or so members of First Church. Abruptly, the door swung open, and a couple I knew to be among the most settled and steady members stepped inside. Both were Sunday school teachers, both held responsible positions, and both were active in the outreach ministry of the church.

As these two drew chairs into the open part of the circle and sat facing Al and me, I stared disbelieving. Although it was summer, the wife huddled in a thick, fur coat. And the husband's hair—in real life, exceptionally dense—had mostly fallen out, leaving him bald except for a few scraggly gray hairs.

Just then, the man to my left started to share something God was teaching him. In an instant, the latecomer was on his feet taking issue with what was said. His wife immediately jumped up to back her husband. Even as their words hung in the air, they were walking out, the woman hugging her heavy coat tightly to her slender body.

It all happened so fast, the group simply sat in stunned silence staring after them. And then, in a flash of insight, I knew: These two people represented what was happening to this church. Once rich and flourishing, First Church was now wasting away, impoverished, smitten by spiritual sparseness, by coldness and hardness of heart. And then it seemed I heard words wrung from the heart of God: "The worst is, they don't even know!"

I was awake now, sobbing.

During the next year, Pastor Torrey went to be with the Lord. We moved out of state, and news filtered to us of different ones leaving the church, among them the Kuhns. Not until we visited the church four years later did we see how devastating the devil's work had been. That Sunday morning, as we left the church parking lot, I turned to my husband. "To think that a church which has given life to so many could become like a morgue!"

"I know," Al agreed. "It's absolutely tragic."

A few weeks later, Eric Kuhn stopped by the house. We talked of the changes since we last visited, of his family, of what happened at First Church. At one point he shook his head. "Sister, no one but God knows the heartbreak my wife and I went through before we left that church."

"But I don't understand," I said. "You fasted and prayed. You wanted God's will. What went wrong?"

He spoke slowly; I felt the pain, the anguish. "We were deceived, my sister . . . we were deceived."

I didn't press for an explanation then. But when I began work on this book, I contacted Eric Kuhn. If someone with his spiritual stature could be deceived, so could anyone. I had to know what was behind his candid but shocking admission. This is what this dear man of God told me.

"At the time we were seeking God's will for a man to replace our beloved pastor, I was under strong oppression from the Enemy. Our son's wife was opposing his ministry; his marriage was breaking up. Then Pastor Torrey gave the leadership to Ted Lytle instead of to Kurt. All the things we had prayed and labored for for many years now broke down over my head. And you know how the devil can elaborate and magnify things.

"Was God so hard that He turned His back on me? Did He shut up heaven and not hear me? Or, had I failed Him? Lord, what is it all about? Many a night my pillow was wet from weeping as I wrestled for answers."

Eric Kuhn went on to explain how, like a man walking against a storm, he was temporarily blinded to the operation of certain forces. He said, "I didn't find out till afterward that a number of influential ones had their minds set on Brother Sparkman because they put the premium on the man most highly educated. Nor did I learn till later that the district superintendent pushed for Brother Sparkman so he could complete his doctorate here at the university. Or that one member hoped for help with his missionary work in Mexico, because Brother Sparkman knew Spanish.

"Besides, behind the scenes, influence favoring Brother Sparkman was brought on Pastor Torrey, at the time a very sick man. And when the secretary brought reports to the board, she always left the impression that more members favored Brother Sparkman than Brother Briggs.

"I think there was another very important factor too," Eric said. "The rebelliousness of those who had been critical of Pastor Torrey's ministry and his emphasis on holiness of life had to be dealt with. Because of my oppression, God allowed me to make the wrong choice. God also allowed the others who were set in what they wanted to make the wrong choice."

Eric Kuhn described the aftermath. "When those who were so strong for Brother Sparkman saw our church going down instead of growing spiritually, and attendance became less and less, they blamed him instead of themselves. They blamed him, too, when their children turned away from the church.

"In some of the best pastors' or Christians' homes, children have been heartaches. This is common. But when anybody wants to shift his guilt on another, this is dishonesty and deceit. An honest mistake, God will forgive, and He understands. But dishonesty, no!"

Not only did the church turn against Pastor Sparkman, but they turned against Eric Kuhn. After the many years the Kuhns had literally laid down their lives for First Church, for the people, and for the ministry, the pain of rejection was like a knife thrust to the heart. Yet Eric Kuhn knew what God required of him—*humility* and *forgiveness*.

One Sunday morning during the communion service, Eric Kuhn stood up in front of the congregation and asked them to forgive him. Stony faces stared back. He was confused. What had he done to cause all this hostility? Only God knew. "There was nothing left for me to do," he told me, "but to resign as elder and leave the church."

And so Satan destroyed the ministry of one of the most spiritual churches I've ever known. To this day, so I am told, First Church remains a spiritual graveyard.

Collective Delusion: Individual Delusion

Deception does not have to take the form of some horrendous heresy to destroy a church. When there is collective delusion—a group deceived about the will of God—the Prince of darkness easily usurps control.

Collective delusion cannot happen, however, unless *individuals* first fall into deception. Satan cannot destroy a church without working through individuals. The trouble is that we tend to understand this in terms of the other fellow—but "not me." The fact is, through unawareness, carelessness, or sheer foolishness, you and I may be guilty of promoting the devil's schemes. How?

1. *We must beware of personal preference.* When praying for guidance, our preferences can muffle God's voice if His preferences differ from ours. Again and again we heard Pastor Torrey say, "In order to know God's will, we must first get to zero."

But did any of us ever get to zero? I wonder. We so cherished Pastor Torrey, we didn't want to consider the possibility of another pastor. Naturally, because of his love and commitment to his flock, Pastor Torrey was reluctant to turn his responsibilities over to another man. Not at all an uncommon situation—a pastor failing to surrender his position soon enough when he becomes too ill to carry on, and his parishioners not ready to relinquish him either.

In such a case, it is difficult for either pastor or people to hear God say that it is time for a change of leadership. Consequently, the church misses God's immediate guidance. To make matters worse, the limitations of the pastor make exploitation of the situation easy for the control-seekers. Positive steps to right the situation are often put off until the church is in desperate straits.

2. *Never shade the truth.* Ironic, isn't it, that Satan gives far more evidence of believing that we reap what we sow than do Christians? Christians so easily shrug off "little" deceptions as trivial. All the while, Satan surely gloats, for even "little" decep-

tions may germinate and yield a whirlwind harvest. Shading the truth or covering up problems inevitably sows fertile seeds of deception.

Even if he is trying to bring about what is plainly God's will, a Christian has no business embracing the Enemy's shifty practices. Our speech is to be forthright, not concealing ulterior motives. To have considered *openly* the benefit of a Spanish-speaking pastor to the missionary's Mexican work, or that the candidate wanted to locate where he could get his doctorate would not have been wrong. The sin was that of pretense and perverted priorities.

3. *Be careful when asking for a sign*. Earlier, I expressed dismay that some members of the board indicated a "sign" was the means by which they came to a decision. I can almost hear someone ask, "So what's wrong with that? Isn't a sign a valid means of guidance? Didn't Gideon put out a fleece to be sure he knew what God was saying? And didn't God honor his asking for a sign?"

True, Gideon used a fleece for guidance, and God did honor it. But the idea was Gideon's, not God's. Maybe one reason God went along with it was that Gideon demonstrated such a mighty faith by the sign he asked God to perform. Not a could-happen-anyway sign. Never would the fleece be wet, the ground dry, or the other way around, if God didn't do it.

But that's not the kind of a sign these people asked for; neither is it the kind of sign most of us employ. We make it easier for God than that. We settle on something more or less improbable, but not something altogether impossible apart from God's intervention. Would we dare stretch our faith to this degree?

Some are not beyond setting up the answer by asking for the unreasonable, the ridiculous. Some things God would never do, even if He wanted to confirm His Word. Neither the unreasonable nor the happen-anyway signs are a reliable means of guidance.

Even a reasonable sign requiring supernatural intervention doesn't rule out the possibility of deception; Satan can and does counterfeit signs and answers. Many are easily fooled into thinking it is God.

Neither should we brush aside the possibility of coincidence. For instance, I remember when friends had a flat tire at an amusement park. The wife took it as a sign that they shouldn't have been there. But my question was, "What about the time we came out of church and found our tire flat?" Certainly God uses circumstances to lead us, but we get into trouble when we depend solely on circumstances for guidance.

If we are willing to be deceived, the Master of Deception will see to it that we get the confirmation we want. Nothing shows us to be a willing prey more than saying, "I want God's will," when in truth we want what we want and finagle any way we can to get it.

4. *When there is a question.* It is always dangerous to ask for something to which God has already said no. Neither is it a light thing to shrug off a clear word from God because of second thoughts. But what if we are sure of divine direction, yet later have misgivings as to what we thought was God's will?

First of all, we need to take a hard look at why we are unsure. Is it because we actually were mistaken? Or is it that now we see another choice would have some greater personal advantage? Or have we been won over by someone promoting some personal cause of his own?

Also, we need to pay heed to the fact that Satan cashes in on pride, selfishness, and problems in the church family. When we are weighed down with heavy concerns, the ensuing mixed-up emotions make us less alert to the Enemy's tricks. Pressure can cause us to misread the signs. Or, as Eric Kuhn pointed out, struggling head down in a swirling storm of stress or opposition, we can easily miss the guideposts altogether.

Being overanxious for the will of God can result in a too hasty decision. On the other hand, if we are afraid to take any step for fear it isn't God's way, we can be prevented from making any decision at all.

Group Dynamics

Often overlooked in a group situation is that the *group process* or *group dynamic* can enable Satan to infuse a whole group with deception by beguiling a single individual.

How does this group process work to create collective delusion? A fundamental law holds that both parties involved in an interaction are modified by the interaction. In other words, the response produced by person A from person B will affect the next response of person A. This idea is basic to the formalized system of group therapy. And the principle applies whether or not persons are Christians: We are being influenced while we are influencing others.

What if one person in a group seeking divine guidance slips into little deceits, stretches the truth, doesn't keep his word, or deliberately plants a false impression? That person, of course, opens himself to deception and the whole group is liable to suffer the consequences.

Another danger. In trying to ascertain God's will in our own personal lives, we carefully pick spiritually mature people for counsel. But within a group situation, we are open to suggestions from all members, spiritually mature or not. We may not realize how much the immature Christian sways our thinking or how much group pressure affects our choices. Neither are some aware that even as the Holy Spirit works through a person to influence others, so can evil spirits.

I am not suggesting that we cannot be rightly influenced, nor that a group is more likely to miss God's guidance than a lone individual. In fact, the group may be a safeguard to being misled. But the dangers which threaten an individual seeking guidance are amplified by the interaction of a group. We need to be on guard.

What about talking over the issues and alternatives with others before making up one's mind as to the right course of action? Fine. Just so whomever we consult is spiritually mature, and the person's number-one priority is to please God. We should back away from anyone who puts a premium on any other thing. And, certainly, to top one's list with "intellectualism" is failing to heed the scriptural warning:

> I will destroy the wisdom of the wise; the intelligence of the intelligent I will frustrate. Where is the wise man? Where is the scholar? Where is the philosopher of this age? Has not God made foolish the wisdom of the world? . . . For the foolishness of God is wiser than man's wisdom, and the weakness of God is stronger than man's strength.[1]

This does not mean that God puts a premium on ignorance or lack of education. The question is, In what (whom) does a person trust? A man with an intellectual approach may be able to give the young people all the right answers, but the Holy Spirit alone is the Source of true wisdom; it is His power operating in a man's life that makes his message effective.

Deception always becomes an imminent danger when we shift our focus from God's resources to man's ability. Of course, total dependency on God must be balanced by responsible action on our part, but we must be on guard lest spiritual accomplishment or high attainment becomes a source of pride.

One of the strongest indictments against pride is that which the prophet Obadiah delivered against the Edomites, descendants of Esau. They were sure that Sola, later known as Petra, their most spectacular and beautiful city, was impregnable. The only access was a two-mile slit in the towering red sandstone cliffs. But Obadiah spelled out judgment:

> "The pride of your heart has deceived you, you who live in the clefts of the rocks . . . who say to yourself, 'Who can bring me down to the ground?' Though you soar like the eagle and make your nest among the stars, from there I will bring you down," declares the Lord. . . . "There will be no survivors from the house of Esau."[2]

And it happened; Edom was reduced to utter desolation. Their allies, their strong position, and the renowned wisdom in which they trusted—none of these things saved them.

Many at First Church had the same proud attitude as the Edomites. They assumed the church was impregnable to the Enemy, and that God would continue to heap blessings upon this congregation—regardless. Wasn't God obligated to sustain the church's high reputation? God wouldn't dare let them call the wrong man as pastor. Their pride gave rise to a false sense of security.

Spiritual pride so easily becomes a mutually reinforced attitude within a group of believers. In an article, "Taking the Spoils from Satan," Ralph Mahoney, president of World MAP, says:

> I have seen too many churches experience great visitations of God and then allow Satan to deceive them into thinking they had achieved some kind of pinnacle. From a pinnacle there is no place to go but down, and that's where they went. Often such a

church, once it has gone into a decline like this, becomes hardened against the gospel, unable to hear the voice of God.[3]

There is no means to evaluate the full effect of deception in any situation. But when any church which has been a powerhouse for God becomes subjugated to the Enemy through pride and deceit, the consequences are fearful.

God's Faithful Remnant

Down through history, God pointed His finger at certain families, cities, and nations; because of their aggregate wickedness, He would utterly destroy them. At the same time his prophets conveyed another message: In the midst of gross wickedness, God has His faithful remnant. Though the nation be destroyed, God would remember those who remember Him. He still does. In the midst of collective delusion, moral and spiritual chaos, God zealously guards those who truly want His will.

Eric Kuhn attests to the reality of God's keeping power. "On those dark days when heaven seemed shut up to my prayers, did God hear me? Of course! He knew that all I wanted was to do His will by being obedient to Him. And all that I did, I did with honesty of heart.

"God saw how the devil sought to shatter our faith, but I could not see it at the time. He also saw my anxiousness; He saw and heard my crying and praying. Oh, yes! God heard me. And above all, He did more than we asked."

God's keeping power was manifest in the way the Kuhns came out on the other side of the battle. Eric Kuhn says, "Now I can sing today, 'Praise God from whom all blessings flow.' "

Any one of us may make a mistake in discerning the will of God. But when we see where we went wrong, there is only one thing to do: admit our mistake openly and honestly to ourselves, to others involved, and to God. If we have had a part in sowing deception, we may suffer some painful reaping. But even so, the humble and contrite person who thoroughly repents of any sin and forgives others will be the recipient of God's redeeming grace. Then there can be a new beginning.

11

Spiritual Therapies or Secular Humanism?

Inner Healing
Psychotherapy
Encounter Groups
Light Meetings

Some years ago, the late Dr. L. Nelson Bell wrote: "Today within the bounds of the Church, we are witnessing a Satanic work of deception and substitution that is intended to deceive even the very elect. This giant hoax is *the substitution of humanism for Christianity.*"[1]

Since those words first appeared in print, the hoax has not diminished; humanism has flourished. Even the charismatic renewal, which some saw as the Holy Spirit's countermeasure against the advance of humanism within organized Christianity, did not halt its progress. In fact, some movements which sprang up within the renewal, inadvertently nurtured the hoax.

At first thought, what could seem more absurd? After all, a genuine work of the Holy Spirit is poles apart from the "no God . . . no belief in the supernatural . . . no uniquely religious emotions and attitudes" position of the humanists. So how could such a thing happen?

Ironically, the spiritual awakening itself precipitated these movements laced with human thought. First of all, the stage was

175

set when the Church, rocked on her heels by the sovereign out-pouring of the Spirit, rediscovered the *holistic* concept of salvation which she had carelessly let slip from her grasp. It became obvious that spiritual rebirth is only the beginning. Forgiveness and cleansing for past sins are not enough—one needs to be made *whole*. Deep emotional scars need healing. A warped personality needs straightening. Garbage accumulated in the subconscious needs to be emptied out. Rooms with locked doors and barred windows in the inner-self need to be opened to the light of God.

Those who experienced the outpouring of the Spirit thus found themselves crying out as did David, "Create in me a clean heart, O God; and renew a right spirit within me."[2] At the same time, sensing human pain and brokenness as never before, they wanted others, too, to be made whole.

This holistic approach to the Christian life provoked a question: *How do we cooperate with the Spirit to bring about wholeness in ourselves and others?*

As Christians struggled for an answer, all sorts of "spiritual therapies" were spawned. Among them, "inner healing" and "light meetings." A flood of prescriptions were doled out: "Get in touch with your feelings"; "Establish and explore intimate loving relationships"; "Share your gut-level feelings, openly, honestly, and unashamedly."

As one after another spiritual therapy became the "in" thing, what began as a work of the Spirit tended to dissipate into works of the flesh. For the most part, these movements were an attempt to blend sound psychological principles and secular therapies with spiritual precepts. But the mixture was subtly tainted with the humanist philosophy that man within himself is capable of self-fulfillment, of ethical conduct, and of creating a utopian society.

Of course, a Christian knows man cannot do it himself. Yet we find it so easy to keep *trying*. That's when Paul's question to the Galatians catches us dead center: "Are you so foolish? After beginning with the Spirit, are you now trying to attain your goal by human effort?"[3]

The Influence of Psychology

Without question, psychology has taught us much about the

human personality; where it often fails is in providing answers. For instance, we can draw on Jung's revelations of the range of human experience and symbolic expression, and his theory of the tensions of complementary opposites in personality. But we learn nothing from him of the work of the Holy Spirit which is so necessary in creating psychic wholeness.

While the mainstream of psychological theories are intrinsically humanistic in their view of life, some are specifically labeled humanistic because of the emphasis on the uniqueness of each human being—his value, dignity, and worth as an individual—and on the interactions that lead to self-actualization.

Take humanistic theorists Carl Rogers and Abraham Maslow, for example. Both have exerted a significant impact on contemporary psychology. Rogers, the father of client-centered therapy, rejected the psychoanalytic view of man as driven by a series of antisocial impulses that he suppresses only with great effort and sacrifice. In Roger's formulation, each human being is viewed as constantly striving toward self-actualization—the full realization of his potential. However, if he is to move toward his goal, he must have warmth and acceptance by others, and similar feelings toward himself. It is not the therapist who "cures" his patient; he merely provides a safe, accepting environment where his client can "cure" himself.

Maslow, like Rogers, began with the assumption that man is innately good and would be able to realize his full potential through fulfilling a hierarchy of needs—first his basic needs of hunger, thirst, sex, and security must be met. Only then can he confront the issues of love, esteem, and self-actualization.

Indeed, there is some truth in these humanistic approaches. We can certainly appreciate the emphasis on loving and caring for the individual. Still, the humanistic view of the *human condition* is directly at odds with what God has revealed about man and his need for redemption.

The more traditional psychodynamic theories, to various degrees, likewise, contradict Christian teaching. Yet while we laugh and say Freud's theory of the Oedipus complex in personality development tells us more about Freud than it does about the rest of us, modern psychology with its humanistic theories and techniques has greatly influenced the Christian perspective.

It is important, then, to grasp the significance of these influences shaping the methods used in Christian counseling and in facilitating Christian growth. Any strategy for change needs to concur with scriptural patterns to achieve inner peace and wholeness. Whatever isn't biblical must be scrapped. Distortions within the various spiritual therapy movements must therefore be identified and reckoned with.

Inner Healing

One such movement taking many cues from analytical psychology is that called "inner healing." Since spiritual conflicts, anxiety, and fears are seen as stemming from traumas, particularly from wrongs done one in the past, an important aspect of the inner healing movement is prayer for healing of the memories.

My first exposure to this sort of prayer came several years ago at a conference where I was to speak. During the conference, a Catholic lay brother concluded his talk with a prayer for healing of the memories. In his prayer he took people back through all the stages of life, including prenatal and preconception stages. I watched to see how people responded.

I saw men and women standing virtually motionless, obviously lost in their memories, tears flowing freely. Later, the young woman standing next to me shared some of the haunting memories the prayer had evoked. But were they healed? I didn't know; only time would tell.

Not long after that, I discovered Agnes Sanford's books. Mrs. Sanford, the wife of an Episcopal priest, told how she was healed by this type of prayer. Prayers for healing of the memories, for inner healing, subsequently became an integral part of her ministry.

About this time, I had a personal experience that added insight into this matter of inner healing.

Some years earlier, when God dramatically touched my life, He gave me the word that my healing would not be instantaneous, but gradual restoration. Though there had not been a specific prayer for healing of the memories, much inner healing had taken place. Yet I knew there were still spiritual conflicts and bondages rooted in the past.

At this particular time, I was bothered by a heaviness of spirit which I couldn't seem to rise above, nor could I pinpoint the cause. Earlier bouts with depression taught me one thing: don't wait to see if it will pass—get help at once. So I made an appointment with the minister who was my spiritual counselor. As is so often the case, insight did not come through talking together; it came through prayer. As I heard him ask God to "heal the pool of sorrow within," there was the sharp inner nudge of the Spirit.

"Pool of sorrow?" . . . As I left his office, and in the days and nights following, those words kept drumming away in my mind. Sensing they had to do with the crux of the problem, I kept asking, "Lord, what does it mean? What are You trying to show me?"

He answered one morning as I sat at my desk praying. Unhappy events from the past came surging into my mind. Quickly I rolled a sheet of paper into my typewriter and began putting them down; the heartbreak of those memories was still sharp enough to bring tears. Afterward I sent the thoughts that had spilled out to my counselor. He wrote back:

> Concerning the pool of sorrow. It appears we have hit upon a very basic part of your problem. For some reason, the pool started early, as you indicated, and has been filling up ever since. Basically, you need healing until the pool of sorrow is turned into a pool of trusting love. I suspect one way is to take all of these memories to the Lord and ask Him to heal them one by one. Your over-identification with those you intercede for is seen in the way you began this way back as a little girl in the situations you mentioned. You have a tremendous ability to identify with anyone in any circumstances, especially if the circumstances are full of hurt and sorrow. . . .
>
> The pool of sorrow must be transformed into a pool of trusting love, probably step by step. Acceptance at a deep level that the God of all love permits suffering and redeems it needs to take hold of you in a tremendous way. All this sorrow isn't just suffering, but it is redeemable by the Lord for His purposes. Your suffering and that of others is not hopeless waste as we let Him redeem it.

—What else did these insights indicate but the need for inner healing!

When I was three, mother taught me the 23rd Psalm. Familiarity had muffled its meaning, but now one phrase lifted off the page: "*He restores my soul.*" In the footnote, I saw, "Or *life*" (Ps. 23:3, RSV). The words were like God's breath upon me. God was redeeming the suffering; He was healing and restoring my life; I dared to believe it!

The Lord had something special, too, to teach me about "trusting love." Part of the heaviness, I now realized, was because I faced a possible move, and memories from the pool of sorrow made it scary. I would never have equated this fear with rebellion, but the Lord did. One day I was stopped short in my Bible reading by what Moses said to the Israelites when they looked across Jordan at the Promised Land and dug in their heels: "If the Lord is pleased with us, he will lead us into that land. . . . Only do not rebel against the Lord. And do not be afraid of the people of the land. . . ."[4] Scared of the giants and the threat of the unknown, the Israelites preferred the security of their miserable existence in Egypt to what God had in mind, which was far better. And their fear became rebellion.

I didn't like the implication. *Me—rebellious?* While I was chewing on that idea, a portion of another verse came to mind: "The rebellious dwell in a dry land."[5] The desert, I well knew, was a miserable place to live.

I turned over a few pages to Psalm 107. Here the psalmist not only graphically traces the consequences of rebellion, but he stresses how God again and again delivers and restores the rebel when he turns from his rebellion to *trust* and *give thanks* for God's unfailing love. And what else? The Lord then turns "the desert into pools of water and the parched ground into flowing springs."[6]

There was only one thing to do: Confess my fear of the future as the sin of rebellion, and choose to trust God for whatever lay ahead. I didn't *feel trusting*—but when I confessed my sin, and by an act of my will chose to trust, the next moment, bubbling up from the depths of my soul, came the song:

Because He lives—I can face tomorrow
Because He lives—all fear is gone
Because I know He holds the future
And life is worth the living, just because He lives.[7]

Oh, yes, I still had to refuse to project memories into the

future of how it had been before in other similar situations. But I was overwhelmed with an amazing certainty: If we should make this move, no matter what lay ahead, I could face it with confidence—*just because Jesus lives!*

In the weeks that followed, as the Spirit continued to dredge up past sorrows, I handed each one over to the Lord. I found that I could not blame the past and nurse the hurts any longer. God was after a "new creation," His likeness in me. The pool was being emptied "step by step." Moreover, as I recommitted myself to trust "the God of all love" for all the future, "trusting love" flowed in to fill the emptiness.

It didn't happen overnight. Years have been involved. Nevertheless, I learned that prayer for healing of the memories is one way God works to restore and make whole. Not *the* way, but *one* way. I am well aware of certain pitfalls in the movement.

For one thing, it is absurd to assume that all spiritual problems are caused by unhealed psychic trauma or by bad treatment in the past. There are other causes needing other remedies. Take the person who is failing to obey God in some matter. Inevitably, any known disobedience saps one's spiritual vitality. All the prayers in the world will not make obedience unnecessary.

Another thing. Bad memories almost always stir bad feelings toward some particular person. We must first deal with any unforgiveness on our part. If we relive in our imagination what caused the hurt, almost surely the face of the one we hold responsible will stand out. Until we move to forgive that person, we cannot expect the memory to be healed.

It's not that those in the inner healing ministry fail to point out the need to forgive everyone who has hurt us. Most do. Still, some who seek help mistakenly think if only the memory would be healed, *then* they could forgive.

True, we may need to draw heavily on God's grace to forgive. But, to forgive is an act of the will. Moreover, you and I have to *live out forgiveness* in the way we respond to our husband or wife, father or mother, brother or sister, child or friend—to anyone who caused or is still causing us pain—today, tomorrow, and the day after that.

There is also the very real possibility, in those situations where we have experienced hurt that we have hurt others. If so, wrongs need to be made right. It is not a prayer ritual we need. We need to decide to say we are wrong and to ask forgiveness—to love and forgive everyone no matter what. When we do, the remembered hurt loses its grip.

Another problem with the inner healing approach is that all unhappy experiences tend to be regarded as bad for us. Actually, what we label bad may have been for our good. We need to be willing to accept the fact that distressing and disappointing events can be God's means of developing character and sensitivity. Unless the "bad" as well as the "good" is accepted and integrated, we will not find wholeness.

What all this comes down to is that prayer for inner healing can be a superficial approach to much deeper problems. It can sidestep personal responsibility—the need to put aside bitterness, the need to forgive, the need to make restitution, the need to take some definite moral action. To relive the pain through picturing the hurtful incidents of the past can produce a highly charged emotional experience. But it does not necessarily produce healing. Unfortunately, a person can mistake the emotional release for a genuine work of the Spirit. This amounts to deception.

Light Meetings

Leaders of "light meetings"—small group sessions where the participants take it upon themselves to expose one another's blind spots—seem to have picked up many cues from contemporary psychology, especially the encounter group movement. Not that group psychotherapy and encounter groups are modern innovations. In fact, the goals and techniques of group psychotherapy have been employed for thousands of years, particularly by religious leaders. Not until the twentieth century, however, were formalized systems of group psychotherapy used for the treatment of large numbers of people suffering emotional and mental disorders. Probably the earliest form of these, appearing shortly after World War I, was psychodrama, a form of therapy in which the patient acts out troublesome situations related to his problem. Said one man, "When I vent my anger through psychodrama, I can be peaceful at the office."

Among the most well-known group sessions instituted within the religious community was the class meeting, conceived by John Wesley, the founder of Methodism. The purpose was to confront and deal promptly with sin and spiritual problems among believers. But the class meetings I remember as a child had by then degenerated into nothing more than a testimony meeting attended by the "faithful few" right after the Sunday morning service; dinner waited in the oven, so let's be brief. If you didn't voluntarily stand up and say how it was with you and the Lord, as in Wesley's time, you still might be called on. But there was no confrontation of sin, and for the most part, the pious went through the ritual of saying what was expected. To have admitted a problem, a need, would have been unthinkable.

Nevertheless, it was the Wesleyan class meeting which gave E. Stanley Jones the idea for the Christian Ashram, a group retreat designed to meet the needs of the people, whatever they might be. Accordingly, the first day at an Open Heart Session, the group was asked, "What do you really need?"

In his autobiography, Jones explains the function of the Open Heart Sessions: ". . . the biggest barriers are within us—fears, resentments, self-preoccupation, guilts, impurities, inferiorities, jealousies, and emptiness. These are the things that separate us from one another, from ourselves, and from God. . . . To bring up your needs and look at them fairly and honestly is halfway to the solution."[8]

He further explains that the group was reminded that some things should not be brought up except in "God's private office." But they were told that if each person was willing to bring up the "more central and less respectable needs, God would guide them to the real needs." All who became involved, he said, soon learned "God's revealings are God's healings."[9]

In recent years, light meetings and similar groups have been founded with a similar intent: to uncover and deal with the sins and weaknesses of persons in the group. In this setting, however, the "revelation" comes not from the person telling his own needs. Rather, it is a session of confrontation. Supposedly getting insights from the Spirit, the group zeros in on the hidden sins and wrong attitudes of one person at a time.

One person I counseled was so depressed after attending several light meetings that she was unable to perform the ordinary tasks of wife and mother. She could neither handle nor put out of her mind the negative remarks made to her. Already lacking self-confidence and any sense of self-worth, she felt all the more of no account.

"Do you see all those things in me that they said were there?" she asked tremulously.

No doubt some of the things she was told were true. But I also knew they were not in her conscious awareness, nor would simply telling her make her aware. Furthermore, I knew she was hanging on my response; a reckless answer could plunge her deeper into depression.

"I can't really say," I told her. "But let me ask you: *Who* does the Bible say is the accuser of the brethren? And *Who* does it say is the Comforter? My Bible says the accuser of the brethren is Satan; the Comforter is the Holy Spirit."[10]

Tears welled up in her eyes. "Oh, thank you," she whispered.

I went on, "Always take to the Lord what someone points out as being wrong. Honestly open yourself to what He says. If the Lord doesn't press the issue, let it drop—for the time anyway. It may mean the problem doesn't exist. Or it may be the Lord knows you aren't ready to handle it right now."

A corporation executive talked with me about his "light meeting" experience. He told how for two hours he was bombarded with accusations of hidden anger. When he strongly rejected the charge, the group retorted, "See, you do have repressed anger!"

"Look" he answered, "I know what I used to be like. And I know God has delivered me from my fiery temper. If He hadn't, right now there would be a person-shaped hole in that wall—and you would be on the outside!"

It is true that Jesus and Paul both say rebuke is in order when a Christian has fallen into sin. But Jesus stresses that the attitude of the one rebuking must be that of infinite forgiveness. Paul, writing Timothy, merged rebuke with encouragement: "Preach the Word . . . correct, rebuke and encourage—with great patience and careful instruction."[11]

Never are we to treat sin with apathy. But if we have reason to confront, we must be careful to communicate forgiveness and inspire trust in God.

One danger in any sort of confrontation is to think because a person has been told his fault, he now has "light." In other words, if we tell a person something he is doing wrong, we assume he no longer has any excuse. We fail to recognize that true conviction is the work of the Holy Spirit. The Spirit alone can reveal the blind spots we all have. True, he uses men and women to expose sin, but unless the Spirit quickens our words to the one we confront, we may cause him to build stronger defenses. In the end, it is that much harder for God to break through.

What's more, just because we see something which needs changing in another doesn't mean God is ready to work on that particular problem at our say-so. Some, confronted by things which they are not ready to cope with, will protect themselves by escaping from reality. This is the last thing we would want to happen.

One of the greatest dangers I see in light meetings is that confrontation can so easily come from the human spirit. When that happens, what is pointed out may be true, but the fault is only symptomatic of something else wrong—something else the Holy Spirit wants to treat first. Too many participants in light meetings want to rush in to do major surgery when a more gentle approach to healing is needed.

I often think how marvelous it is that God doesn't confront us with everything that needs changing in one session. How grateful I am that at the lowest point in my life, He chose to heal through a "restoration process"! Contributing to my illness were deep psychological and emotional scars, deep-seated, lifelong attitudes that were distortions of reality, and strong negative habit patterns. Had God faced me with the whole mess in one flash of time, I'm convinced a tremendous explosion would have fragmented me into a million pieces.

Instead, tenderly and lovingly, God began to restore me to health. Oh, yes, a measure of deep healing took place immediately following that dynamic divine touch. Where there had been nothing but blackness and despair, light was spilling in, and there was hope. I *knew* I was on my way to wholeness.

Still, the restoration process, the renewal goes on—and on! Sometimes slowly, and I say, "Hurry up, Lord!" But then, when God deals with some issue in a whirlwind, I beg Him to slow down. Either way He works to "create in me a clean heart . . . and renew a right spirit within me." And that's what I want more than anything.

Now here's an exciting thought. David does not pray for God to *cleanse* his heart. Rather he prays for God to *create* within him a clean heart. Cleansing has to do with past sins, but creation has to do with bringing something brand-new into existence. In the beginning, God created man from the dust of the earth. But the heart—or mind—is continually *recreated* through the input of all experience; what we think and do is constantly integrated into a "new" mind. It is an ongoing process—God taking the dust of human thought and experience and creating a clean heart and restoring a right spirit as we yield to the work of His Spirit in our lives.

By his life and words, the Apostle Paul appealed to fellow believers to present their bodies to Christ as "living sacrifices." And He urged, "Be transformed by the renewing of your mind."[12] This is not some elusive ideal; Paul pointed to the practical ways to express outwardly one's inner commitment. For your mind to be renewed, he said, this is how you should think and act, and in the following verses he outlined *how* we are to use the gifts God has given us.

It is the call to be "living sacrifices," and the need of spiritual metamorphosis effected by the Holy Spirit as we walk in daily obedience, which I see as missing from inner healing, encounter groups, and light-meeting movements. Unfortunately, many are fooled into thinking these things are not essential. Living in this deception, they give little evidence of the Christ life.

Loving Relationships—Is There a Limit?

The renewed attention to holistic salvation has spawned another movement which may be the most dangerous and deceptive of all the popular spiritual therapies. This movement stresses not only the need for uncovering hidden areas of the soul, but the need to discover and assert one's "authentic self." Those who push this approach say that if we are to become authentic persons, we must be able to express our uniqueness in whatever way we feel comfortable. And one of the most effective ways to do this is to explore intimate loving relationships where nothing is held back.

The line of reasoning behind this approach is something like this: There is a universal cry within every man, woman, boy, and girl—the cry, "Please love me!" That cry, for the most part, goes unheard or ignored by the Church corporately, and by Christians individually. The reason Christians do not often respond to this cry for love and acceptance is that they cannot cope with the brokenness, the sin and darkness in another's soul. Therefore, it is important for each of us to find one other individual with whom we can be totally open and transparent, who will accept us just as we are, and who will commit himself or herself to reciprocal openness.

There is no question that we all need close friends with whom we can share at a deeply personal level. But exploring intimacy with anyone but our marriage partner poses hazards.

It may come as a shock to some that the most intimate experience a couple can have is not the physical act of sex. The most intimate experience a couple can have is in sharing deeply personal spiritual perceptions and goals, and in praying and worshiping God together. At the same time, this sort of intimate experience stimulates emotional sensibility and can heighten sexual awareness. For the married couple, that's a big plus. But when any two people covenant to explore intimacy outside the bonds of marriage, they inevitably walk head-on into subtle and powerful temptation. The road to heaven is strewn with the wreckage— broken people who started out as "soul mates," as "special" brothers or sisters in the Lord (with the other or same sex), even as "prayer partners," but ended up sexually involved. When this happens, faith is often abandoned, and the person sinks deeper and deeper into sin.

Most of us know what it is to meet a fellow believer and immediately feel a mutual attraction that is sheer magnetism. Spiritual affinity, it is called. In itself, this is not necessarily wrong. It is wrong, however, if either one exploits those feelings by undue familiarity.

We need to keep in mind that a genuine move of the Spirit in our lives usually heightens the emotions. The same nervous system which responds to sexual stimuli responds to religious stimuli. This is essentially why pagan tribal religious rites turn into sexual orgies or at least include sexual pantomime. It is crucial that we not ignore the strength of human sexual desires, which can be unexpectedly triggered in the most spiritual atmosphere when we meet someone for whom we have a strong spiritual attraction.

I was unhappily reminded of how deceptive spiritual affinity can be when I learned of the breakup of one young couple. With problems which hadn't been resolved in five years of marriage, the two were an easy mark for Satan. It happened at a "Jesus rally." While everyone was freely embracing and saying, "I love you," both found themselves experiencing feelings for persons of the opposite sex unlike any they had ever felt for each other. Apparently they had no understanding of the forces involved. In the end, they decided if they couldn't have those same feelings for each other, this was another reason to end the marriage.

They ignored the scriptural teaching concerning love and commitment, to say nothing about divorce. They let physical feelings influence moral choices, rather than adhering to God's standard for righteous living, and played right into the hands of the Deceiver.

There is another question that needs to be dealt with: Why had this couple never had these same feelings toward each other? Actually, this isn't unusual, nor should it be surprising if we remember that the most intimate experience one can have is sharing deeply spiritual feelings.

Unfortunately, few Christian couples share at a deeply spiritual level with each other, even those who can talk about other matters easily. Why? Because every one of us has inconsistencies in our lives; we know they are there; we know those closest to us know they are there. Our imperfections loom up to inhibit our sharing about spiritual things. We are afraid we won't be taken seriously, or that later we will be reminded when we are less than what we have shared. And since we all are prone to protect the religious part of our being, we tend to keep our spirit closed to those who might react negatively.

It is different when we are among strangers who reach out to us with loving acceptance. They haven't seen us at our worst, so we feel freer to open up our spirits, to share our spiritual awareness, insights, and convictions. In a setting, then, where everyone is worshiping the Lord openly, where there is a special move of the Spirit, where love feelings are flowing freely, one easily encounters spiritual intimacy and affinity. The one who doesn't understand the dynamics of this attraction is apt to think what he or she has in marriage is shoddy by comparison. And married or not, one can misconstrue physical feelings to be a spiritual encounter. Preoccupation with emotions, or focusing on feelings when making decisions, is always a dangerous practice.

We also need to look at the hazards created by the widespread push for unrestrained openness. What this practice often comes to is, "I'll share all my garbage with you, and you share all your garbage with me." The upshot is that two people simply end up with twice as much garbage.

Certainly, the Bible teaches that righteousness and honesty go hand in hand. We are to be transparent before God, and in a sense, before men. But basically, honesty and transparency in the Scriptures has to do with avoiding fraudulent business practices and being a phony. We are not to pretend to be something we are not, or profess one thing and live something else.

Openness and learning to trust are core concepts of the encounter group movement. But it was the "Jesus freaks" of the sixties, a youth culture revolting against a plastic society and the pharisees in the Church, that began calling Christians to openness. Somehow the idea caught on that openness meant "letting it all hang out," and that was considered spiritual. Many who were persuaded to share their most intimate feelings later had bitter regrets.

This happens often on the Christian college campus. I'm at once apprehensive when a girl comes to me ecstatic after spending hours "sharing" with a "new brother in the Lord." I know what I will hear: "He was really open with me, and I could really be open with him." I know how it was: "Trust me," the young man urged. The girl, flattered that someone cared enough to listen and caught in the mood of the moment, spilled out a lot of personal things which would have been far better kept to herself or shared with a mature Christian woman.

I also know how it probably will end. The girl will be shattered when confidence is betrayed, or when the young man simply brushes her off and finds someone else with whom to be open.

What the girl, and perhaps the boy, too, doesn't fully realize is that this sort of openness can be a form of sexual sublimation. It can also lead to sexual intimacy. In any case, it's important to use discretion; one shouldn't go around sharing everything with everybody.

The emphasis on intimate relationships in order to become an authentic person has another inherent evil. Romans, chapter one, depicts the sordid consequences when people turn from worshiping the *Creator* to serve and worship the *creature*. In effect, this is what we do when we try to draw out of a human relationship what only God can be to us. And how we do try!

Christians have been caught in the push for getting the most for *oneself* out of all relationships. And due to the preeminence of the marriage relationship, there has been an avalanche of books and tapes on how to seduce one's mate and enjoy perpetual peak sexual performance. But with all the attention given to making one's sex life sizzle, many have lost sight of the *Creator of sex*, the beauty of mutual love; they are giving themselves to their own pursuit of pleasure.

Even men and women from conservative church backgrounds are off and running in search of the ultimate sexual experience. And that means, within marriage anything goes—as long as it is mutually agreeable. No boundaries. No norm.

To be sure, many Christians needed to be freed from thinking marital sex is subspiritual. Some needed to see this way of communication of commitment and caring as ordained by God. And the prudish needed to be told that God intended sex to be fun.

Some needed to hear that making love is not always the same; it may be serious or hilarious, a calm delight or wildly ecstatic joy, cozy belonging or all giving. But whatever the mood, sexual relations are God's gift to marriage to be enjoyed with thanksgiving. Christian sex manuals have said these things clearly, and that is good.

Still, the emphasis on sexual gratification has put a strain on many marriages. In many cases it has created unrealistic expectations. Countless couples have been jolted to find that sizzling sex by itself can't carry a marriage through the sure-to-come low points. As family historian Edward Shorter observes:

> The intensification of the couple's erotic life . . . has injected a huge chunk of high explosive into their relationship . . . to the extent that erotic gratification is becoming a major element in the couple's collective existence, the risk of marital dissolution increases.[10]

The most troubling aspect of this preoccupation with sex, the press to explore intimate relationships, as well as the inner-healing and light-meeting movements, is that man becomes the center, the means of his own salvation. In all of this, of course, we see the influence of secular humanism.

The Christian gospel gives first priority to *reconciliation to God and relationship with God* made possible through Jesus Christ. The gospel of humanism, on the other hand, focuses on man's *reconciliation to man*—and it is *all up to man*.

The truth is, not one of us can realize our full potential apart from God. Not only is our eternal destiny determined by our reconciliation to God and relationship with God—but so is wholeness, Christian maturity, and fruitfulness.

By My Spirit

The Bible states that it is God's eternal purpose to transform us into the image of His Son—ultimate wholeness. But it is the work of the Holy Spirit to effect that change. Likewise, it is only as the Spirit works through us that we can effectively help others. The danger with all the various spiritual therapies we have discussed is that men and women take on the role of the Spirit, but they are using merely human techniques.

It's not that the methods copied from secular psychology are all bad, nor that God doesn't use them. But all too often, the techniques and methods are not surrendered to the leading and power of the Holy Spirit.

I've seen it happen, too, that God gives a certain individual a unique and distinct way of helping others. But when someone else copies that ministry, it goes awry. We can learn from others, but we have to be careful not to pick up someone else's distinctive calling.

Another mistake we make: if we find something works well in helping a number of people, we apply it wholesale. But Jesus never locked himself into a formula; He didn't minister to people that way. He said, in every situation, "I do only what I see my Father do."[14]

The same sensitivity and commitment to the Father's will allows us to use many of the same techniques used by secular therapists without becoming part of "the giant hoax, the substitution of humanism for Christianity."[15]

But whatever approach we take to wholeness in Christ, we need to mark it well: *maturity takes time.* And the Lord God Almighty has declared His purposes are accomplished, *"not by might nor by power, but by my Spirit."*[16] If we try to do it ourselves, we will end up with a superficial renewal and think we have achieved reality.

12

What Really Happens When We Die?

It is one thing to read Paul's warning that the devil masquerades as an angel of light. It is quite another to observe firsthand Satan playing this role. Most often he shows himself through his servants, men and women who "masquerade as servants of righteousness" and "apostles of Christ."[1] Seldom does he appear as a bright shining creature or as some semblance of illumination. But he can. I know.

It happened when my husband and I were students in Bible school, near the end of the first year. As a family with three children, we had moved into a communal-living fellowship and the pressures resulting were more than we were prepared to handle: pressures of schoolwork, pressures at work, pressures to be a family when the system was not geared for a family as students. Of course the devil got into the act, blowing the whole matter out of proportion.

But what could I do? Our lives were very much controlled by the decisions of others, decisions which sometimes baffled me. Three years of this? We'd never survive as a family! Why didn't anyone understand? Why didn't anyone seem to care?

The more I wrestled with these questions and tried to cope with the children's feelings of insecurity and rejection, the more submerged I became in dark fears, in feelings of hopelessness and despair. I knew the only way out of the darkness was to surrender the hurts and the confusion to the Lord, and to accept those things over which I had no control. But I had allowed my mind to become locked in a battle with all the wrongs which caused hurt to our family. And the darkness moved in until I tottered precariously on the edge of a total breakdown.

Then one night, utterly exhausted by the mental and emotional pain of depression, I turned the light out and sat alone in the darkness of our room. Suddenly, I "saw" the room before me glowing with light. I was outside the light, but within its spread there was an aura of warmth, of comfort, of tranquillity. This wondrously soothing state of peace was being offered to me by some "presence." I could be free of the tormenting thoughts, the mental depression. All I had to do was stop struggling—stop reaching out to God. Stop now!

This was not a *surrender to* the Lord. Rather, a giving up God—just *letting go* of Him. A choice, it seemed, I could make in a split second, which would immediately and forever free me from the torment, the depression, the darkness.

There isn't any way to describe the attraction of that light with the release it offered. Only for a brief flash did I sense an impending doom.

I was so tired . . . so tired of the struggle . . . and the light promised rest . . . rest . . . I had to have rest. . . .

Suddenly, crashing into my thoughts, I heard as it were God's warning shout, "He comes as an angel of light!"

Satan! Of course. It was Satan appearing as an angel of light. My reaction was swift. "Jesus! Protect me by Your blood. . . . In the name of Jesus, Satan, get out!"

With that, he was gone.

I sat for some time, stunned and shaken. I was not so much frightened as confounded at Satan's guise. I would never have believed he could offer comfort and light and peace, and make the counterfeit so real, so desirable. To someone who was not a Christian, maybe, but not to me.

Beyond Death's Door

I always feel a bit smug when God turns one of the Enemy's tricks to our advantage. That's what He did for me; He turned Satan's luminous illusion into a genuinely enlightening experi-

195

ence. It would be over fifteen years before I would read the *Reader's Digest* condensation of the book *Life After Life* by Dr. Raymond A. Moody, Jr. But having been exposed to Satan's power of imitation, I was more adequately fortified against possible deception. I wasn't fooled for a moment as to the identity of the "being of light"; I'd already encountered the Prince of darkness masquerading in this form.

Yet others would be captivated by these "new insights." It was a disturbing thought. How many would believe the lie that this is what life after death is really like—equally pleasant for saint and unredeemed sinner, so what's there to worry about?—and end up in hell?

As one would expect, Christians were soon debating the book. What I did not expect was to hear so many say, "Surely this being of light was Christ—who else?" If they had opened their Bibles and carefully checked out these "new insights," they would have known *"who else!"*

For those who may not be familiar with the book, Moody studied approximately 150 cases of people who came near to death or who clinically died and were then revived. Although there were variations, each had a strikingly similar story to tell. From the common feelings and events reported, Moody constructed an "ideal" or theoretical model. Essentially, it is as follows:

Shortly after hearing himself pronounced dead, the patient feels himself float out of his body and hears a loud disturbing noise as he swishes through a long, dark tunnel. Suddenly, he is looking down on his body, watching the resuscitation attempt. Spirits of deceased relatives and friends come to help him.

A loving warm spirit—a being of light—appears. This being questions him, nonverbally, as to what he has done with his life—not for the purpose of judgment, but simply as a learning experience. At the same time, he is presented an instant replay of his life.

Approaching a barrier, he finds he must return to earth. "Overwhelmed by intense feelings of joy, love, and peace," he does not want to return, but something pulls him back, and he is reunited with his physical body. The person's life is remarkably changed by the experience, particularly in that he no longer fears death. Since words are inadequate to describe this episode, and because others scoff, he is reluctant to discuss his experience.[2]

In his later study, Moody found "several new elements" which he discusses in *Reflections on Life After Life*. But they occurred far less frequently than those referred to above.

What we find, then, is Moody and other researchers agreeing that the one most commonly shared element has been an encounter with the being of light. This also proves to be the element most profoundly affecting the individual.

Surely, for the Christian evaluating these experiences, this is the most crucial element. One cannot accept the information intimated by this light-being, along with the conclusions drawn by individuals reporting this experience, and at the same time accept the authority of the Bible.

Even if this being of light was not suspect, I would have to reject this ideal model. I simply cannot accept the suggestion that all near-death or after-death experiences are so inexpressibly blissful. Not that I question Moody's accuracy in reporting these testimonies, but life itself has taught me differently.

First of all, there is the story my mother told. Though only a child at the time, she never forgot the horror of a dying neighbor's screams. With every breath, he begged to be pulled up in bed, shrieking that his feet were already in the flames of hell.

And there was the terrible end of Brother Macy. This old man held some sort of record for the number of years he served as Sunday school superintendent of the small rural church we attended when I was a child.

What sticks with me is the picture of a squat little balding man in a collarless black suit, looking at me through round wire-rim glasses. And close beside him, his elfinlike wife with wisps of gray hair slipping free from the soft little bun on the back of her head—friskily rebelling against the puritanical plainness of her long-sleeved black cotton dress with its long skirt mostly hiding her heavy black stockings. Even as a child, I was impressed; the Macys looked *so* religious. Only one item of the couple's garb was not black. Brother Macy's shirt was white—collarless, too, of course. Wearing a necktie would have been sinful.

But there was nothing saintly or euphoric about Brother

Macy's death. He died screaming that he was dropping into hell. The church people were stunned. But when anyone said, "How unbelievable!" Mother only looked grim. Years later, I learned what she knew. Sister Macy told her some time before the old man's death that the goats her husband kept were a constant sexual temptation to him. Apparently the rigid mode of dress and pious ways were a cover-up for the rottenness underneath that he had never dealt with. In the end, the dying man faced the stark reality of how grossly he had deceived himself.

Closer to home, there was the death of my uncle who had lived his whole life by his own rules. Only when he was refused government family relief checks did he legally marry the woman who bore him five children. Nobody, but nobody was going to tell Uncle Harry what to do! And God? As far as we know, he never acknowledged God's existence.

Then came the telephone call that he was dying. When my parents arrived at the hospital, they found a terrible scene. My uncle, propped up in bed, stared straight ahead at something only he could see, his face contorted in a look of sheer horror. At times he pushed himself forward as if straining to see more closely whatever it was that terrified him so. If one of his daughters would start to enter the room, one look at her father and she would rush out the door. The nurses refused to stay in his room. Whatever my uncle saw at the last, it certainly came nowhere close to Moody's ideal model of near-death experiences.

And I knew of one more case that ran contrary to this theoretical model. My father's first marriage ended when his wife, Fay, died of blood poisoning. Dad was left with two small children, a stack of bills, and a mother-in-law who was an avowed atheist, causing no end of trouble. When the children visited her, she encouraged them to do things Dad expressly forbade. When Dad remarried, she turned them against their stepmother. It was an ugly situation. But I think it was her mocking God that caused Dad to finally put a stop to all visits.

By the time of her death Dad had had no contact with her for some years. Weeks after her funeral, an in-law, hounded by the memory, came to tell my father that the old lady had died screaming for him. She knew she was on her way to hell; she had a terrible confession to make; she must see my father. But her family had scoffed at the whole idea and stubbornly refused to call him.

These near-death episodes caused me to think that an elusive factor had escaped Moody's attention. Then I read the book *Beyond Death's Door* by Maurice Rawlings, M.D., a man with top credentials to write about this subject.[3] Particularly intriguing to me was what Rawlings saw as the missing component, why the stacked "research" discounted the idea of judgment and hell.

While resuscitating a terrified patient who told Rawlings he was actually in hell, and who begged the doctor to pray for him and not let him die, Rawlings was jolted into considering that death was not the painless extinction he had believed. He was also jolted into reading his Bible to find out what hell was supposed to be like. He discovered that and more—a compelling personal faith in the Bible as veritable truth and the reality of Jesus Christ as his own Savior and Lord.

As he began his study of after-death experiences, he wondered how it was that, except for cases of attempted suicide, all the published reports of Doctors Elizabeth Kübler-Ross, Karlis Osis, Elendur Haraldsson, and Moody represented unbelievably good experiences. That there were no bad experiences did not square with what he learned from interrogating patients he personally had resuscitated. Upon contacting other doctors, he found that they, too, had had bad experiences reported to them. Why, then, did the above researchers unearth only these one-sided accounts?

His first clue came from the man who said he was in hell. Before becoming stabilized, this patient suffered three or four episodes of clinical death. During one of these episodes, he "saw" his mother and stepmother in a very lush and beautiful valley illumined by a brilliant beam of light. The man's mother had died when he was fifteen months old. He had never seen a picture of her. Yet weeks later, he was able to pick her picture out from among several others. He also recalled other particulars—standing aside and watching the doctor and nurses working over his body lying on the floor, the prayer the doctor had led him to say, and other details of his after-death experience that were *pleasant*. Earlier, when Rawlings asked him to recall what he saw in hell, he expressed surprise. *He remembered nothing whatsoever of the hell he had described while being resuscitated two days earlier.*[4]

"Apparently," says Rawlings, "the experiences were so frightening, so horrible, so painful, that his conscious mind could not cope with them; and they were subsequently suppressed far into his subconscious." This leads him to theorize, "When patient interviews are delayed in any way, this may allow enough time for the good experience to be mentally retained and reported by the patient and the bad experiences to be rejected or obliterated from recall."[5]

Rawlings points out that Moody and other investigators who are psychiatrists collect their data after some time has elapsed. Not so with him. "As a cardiologist working with critically ill patients in the coronary care units of several hospitals," he is involved in fighting for the life of the patient while his "data" is happening. This, he believes, is why he hears as many bad experiences as good ones. If patients were interviewed "while they are still in trouble and calling for help and before the experience can be forgotten or concealed," Rawlings surmises, "researchers would find bad experiences to be as frequent as good ones."[6]

It is an established fact that the conscious mind can repress or block out horrifying scenes so that they are beyond recall. If this is what happens with certain patients, it could certainly account for the dearth of bad experiences reported. At any rate, I found Rawlings' book in agreement with my own much more limited observations: Dying persons apparently do have glimpses "beyond death's door." And what some see is far from pleasant.

But what if there was not a single account of any such hellish experience? No matter. Regardless of how the "evidence" is stacked, Paul's words thunder down through the ages: "Let God be true, and every man a liar!"[7]

When I read in God's Word that "man is destined to die once, and after that to face judgment,"[8] and God "will punish those who do not know God and do not obey the gospel of our Lord Jesus . . . with everlasting destruction,"[9] I can only conclude that those who say, "I've been there and back, and it makes no difference how a person lives," are victims of satanic deception. Being ignorant of the devil's genius at counterfeit, these patients simply take for granted that a being of light appearing at death must be Christ. Or God. Unfortunately, many who read their reports jump to the same conclusion.

This association springs from the term *light* used often throughout the Scriptures as a symbol for God—and from Jesus' claim, "I am the light of the world."[10] Yet on one occasion, Jesus went on to say, "I am going away. . . . Where I go, you cannot come. . . . If you do not believe that I am the one I claim to be, you will die in your sins."[11]

But is this the message communicated by the figure Moody's patients described? Hardly! No matter what their answer to the question, "What have you done with your life?" they felt only total love and acceptance from the light. Even when "their most apparently sinful deeds were made manifest," they insisted this being responded not with anger or condemnation, but rather "with understanding and even with humor."[12]

God is love—that's the why of Calvary. Certainly He understands our weaknesses—that's why He offers us His strength. But He offers us no assurance, whatever, if we walk through life spurning His love. Quite the opposite. The Bible plainly says, "He [God] has set a day when he will judge the world with justice by the man he has appointed. He has given proof of this to all men by raising him [Jesus] from the dead."[13] And Jesus speaks candidly of that day when He will be forced to say, "Depart from me, you who are cursed, into the eternal fire prepared for the devil and his angels. . . . Then they will go away to eternal punishment. . . ."[14]

The proposition, therefore, that God sees sin as humorous, or that hell is simply a "learning experience," is sheer madness! And to swallow that lie is to be cruelly deceived.

So who is this being of light at the end of the tunnel?

I do not question that in some cases this being is none other than the Lord Jesus Christ. Those who were with my grandmother's brother when he was dying told how his last hours were spent talking with Jesus and joyously greeting loved ones who had gone before.

But in many cases, having myself experienced the frightening reality of Satan's ruse as an angel of light, I believe that some-times it is the Master Deceiver in his most subtle form—passing himself off as a look-alike for the One who said, "I am the Light of the World." Stephen Board points out, "It is not surprising for old Lucifer to assume that disguise, for his name literally means light bearer and his pre-Adamic effulgence was dazzling."[15]

Remember Paul's concern that the Galatian Christians were "turning to a different gospel—which is really no gospel at all." He warned that they should not be taken in "even if we or an an-gel from heaven should preach a gospel other than" the gospel of Christ.[16]

There is no question about it. The message the counterfeit be-ing of light communicates is an absolute denial of Christ's gospel. The dying are led to believe there is no need for repentance, no need for reconciliation with God, no need for any concern other than to love others and gain knowledge. This, more than any-thing else, positively identifies this impostor as Satan. Here again is the same Big Lie by which Satan beguiled Eve to eat of the tree of knowledge: With such knowledge, you will be like God; you can do as you please without fear of judgment; you can sin and get away with it; you will not die. Satan, posing as an an-gel of light, thus swaddles the dying person in a security blanket as sleazy as cobwebs. But more, he seals the individual off from knowing the only One who can legitimately remove the fear of death.

Dr. Elizabeth Kübler-Ross

One of the most passionate voices peddling Satan's death-and-dying propaganda during the last decade has been that of Dr. Elizabeth Kübler-Ross. Recently, I picked up a magazine and read how a young mother, dying of cancer, and her family, were helped by "The Death-and-Dying Lady." It was a moving story, reflecting the sensitivity and concern Kübler-Ross demon-strates to the terminally ill.

But it was also the story of a doctor whose comfort to the dy-ing reeks with deception. As I read, I felt I was watching a seda-tive administered to a woman about to enter the gas chamber at Dachau, a scene in which the guard smilingly reassures the woman that she is just going to the showers before being issued new clothing and sent to a lovely resort for rest and recuperation. But the lie did not wipe out the terrible reality on the other side of the door. Nor does the false assurance inspired by Kübler-Ross change the fate of those who go through death's door without having made peace with God.

The dreadful fact is that Kübler-Ross has drawn many adherents from the ranks of those who call themselves followers of Christ. Why can't they see through the devil's ploy? This question prodded me to look more closely at how Christians could be so deceived.

Following the publication of her book, *On Death and Dying* (1969), in which she described the five stages of death—denial, anger, bargaining, depression, acceptance—Elizabeth Kübler-Ross quickly became a worldwide authority on the psychological aspects of death.[17] Few people realized Kübler-Ross's growing involvement in the occult. In fact, just before publication of the book, she claims a patient of hers showed up following her death and burial "as her fully human self," to thank the doctor for having taken care of her, and to encourage her to continue her work with dying patients.[18]

Until then, Kübler-Ross had been sure death was oblivion. But soon after, she was saying she had changed her view; there *is* life after death. The change, she said, came about from her observations of dying patients and from interviews with those who survived clinical death. The change had nothing to do with God. As far as Kübler-Ross is concerned, God does not exist.

A short time later, Kübler-Ross began having out-of-the-body experiences having nothing to do with death. She believes this phenomenon, known as astral projection, duplicates the sort of separation from the body that takes place at death.

Though her first OOBE was "spontaneous," she turned to Robert A. Monroe, author of *Journeys Out of the Body*, to learn how to leave her body on command. According to Kübler-Ross, in no time, she was able to zoom out of her body. She recounts how, during one of her early experiences, she found herself traveling faster than the speed of light—horizontally. She says, "I switched and made a right-angle turn, rounded a big hill and went up . . . to a place so far that when I came back . . . *I felt like a beaming source of light that could illuminate the darkest corner of the world.*"[19] (Emphasis mine.)

But wait! The Bible clearly states that *we who are Christ's disciples are light because we have the Light of Life.*[20] We are to shine before men, illuminating the darkness of an evil world. Apart from Christ, this function can be nothing but Satan's counterfeit.

Since Satan's imitations include a spurious conversion, it is not surprising that Kübler-Ross talks about her "rebirth." It began, she says, as another OOBE in which she went through "every single death of every single one of my thousand patients . . . the physical pain, the dyspnea, the agony, the screaming for help. . . . 10,000 more deaths wouldn't have made any difference, since all the pain you could endure was already there anyway." The moment she totally accepted the pain, it disappeared. And there followed "the most incredible rebirth experience. . . . It was so incredibly beautiful. . . ." The next morning, she walked outside and found herself "in love with every leaf, every tree, every bird—even the pebbles."[21]

These mystical experiences gave rise to her teaching that "Shanti Nilaya" is "the ultimate home of peace" where we all end up one day after we have come to accept all the agonies of life. And that the only "hell" after death is "self imposed and self-inflicted" as we are forced to review our lives and see how our "lower rather than higher choices" affected ourselves and others.[22]

The "evidence" Kübler-Ross presents at lectures and workshops to prove the spirit lives on includes stories about her "loving spooks." It is common, she says, for her to witness the physical materialization of spirit beings. A tape recording she plays sounds like two men singing. Not so, she says. One is a male friend, but the other is "Willie," one of her three main personal spirit guides.[23]

Kübler-Ross, denying the divinity of Christ, placed herself theologically among spiritists at the very beginning of her quest to gain knowledge of life after death. Her research was bound to lead to spiritist practices. Failing to recognize the possibility of satanic deception, she would have been extremely susceptible to the influence of evil spirits.

God strictly forbids His people to have anything to do with a person involved in spiritism or the occult (except, of course, to bring them deliverance). So for anyone taking the Bible seriously, the teachings of Kübler-Ross are clearly off-limits. Still, Christians heedlessly skip over where her "evidence" is coming from, and look to her as an authority on the afterlife.

When a review of nine books dealing with death appeared in *Christianity Today*, reviewer Dale Saunders observed that six of the nine, "all bow, more or less deeply," to Kübler-Ross.[24] Just last night, while reading a Christian writer I greatly admire, I was stopped short by her reference to "the great" Kübler-Ross. What's more, on my desk lies a notice of a conference on suicide designed to "unmask the myths," and "directed to the survivors of suicide, doctors, pastors, counselors, therapists, and laypeople." It is a conference featuring Kübler-Ross and sponsored by the institute bearing the name of a well-known minister. I stare at the ad and feel crumpled inside.

Time magazine (Nov. 12, 1979) carries the story: "The conversion of Kübler-Ross from thanatology to séances and sex." The word is, Kübler-Ross "has apparently lost any remaining credibility with her professional colleagues. The reason: her close association with Jay Barham, who claims to be a psychic and conducts séances that include intercourse between participants and 'entities' from the spirit world."[25]

The story, with all of its vulgarities, presents the inevitable results of satanic deception. It seems there is no limit to delusion once a person gives himself to lies.

How have Kübler-Ross adherents reacted to *Time*'s exposé? Many, I imagine, are still groaning, "But how could we know!"

True, they could not have known about the "séances and sex." But a parade of clues should have alerted Christians to the deception of Kübler-Ross's canon. The most significant clue is that Kübler-Ross gives no credence to the personhood of God, to Jesus Christ as the Son of God, or to the Bible as the Word of God. Scorning any biblical revelation, she has built her case for immortality on her own "findings." And the Bible sounds an alarm to beware of anyone who seeks to penetrate the veil of death and discover knowledge of the spirit world apart or beyond what God has revealed in His Word.

Why did Christians fail to heed the warning signals?

It happens all the time when a warm, eloquent person actively communicates caring and compassion; the "good" tends to cancel out the heresies being expounded. Kübler-Ross was seen to fill the need of the dying to have someone with whom to share their anxieties, fears, and hopes, without having to pretend everything's okay. That she dealt them the ultimate unkindness by consoling the dying with her diabolical delusions was disregarded.

Adding to the impact is the certainty with which she speaks. Let someone—especially "a somebody"—say, "I know beyond a shadow of a doubt. . . !" and people—especially those uncertain about the matter—are prone to believe that person must be right.

This is a delusion of course. A statement is not true just because it is spoken in italics and exclamation points. Yet this delusion has trapped scores of persons possessed by feelings of uncertainty and doubts about the hereafter.

Robert M. Herhold, a Lutheran pastor who attended a series of lectures given by Kübler-Ross before a group of clergymen, reflects, "Several pastors commented later on how reassuring her words were."[26] Apparently, no one discounted the message as being contrary to the Bible or questioned the messenger's method of arriving at her beliefs. Nor did these clergymen question among themselves as to why they needed this sort of reassurance.

Herhold admits that at first he, too, felt reassured, but he began to be troubled by the fact that what they had been offered was "a human-centered immortality fortified by stories of patients who have 'died' and reported back." There was not "a hint that God may be what eternal life is all about." He goes on to say:

> To be sure, many of us are more interested in having more time or more creativity, or more of something else after death than we are in God. *But it is precisely the God question which concerned Jesus*: "And this is eternal life: for men to know you, the only true God, and to know Jesus Christ, whom you sent."[27]

Indeed, it is precisely the God question that should concern us. *To know Him*—and the Greek verb indicates progression—*IS eternal life.* It is through Jesus that we come to know God redemptively. There is no basis for hope of eternal life if one sidesteps the crucified and risen Christ who came to reveal the Father—no matter what Kübler-Ross says.

But then, as Herhold points out:

> Many of us clergy are guilty of Kübler-Ross's error. We try to relate people to life after death when we should be relating them to God. It is the presence of God which gives eternal life its content. Paul does not celebrate our endless existence; rather he celebrates the fact that nothing can separate us from the love of God.[28]

Those of us who say we are Christians and have been taken in by "a human-centered immortality" cannot blame Moody, Kübler-Ross, or anyone else. The fault is our own. It is in looking for answers apart from God, apart from obedience to the Word, apart from meeting God's conditions that we get into trouble. If we are not to become an easy mark for Satan's fallacies, we must keep God at the center of our spiritual quest—always.

We must never forget that every work of Christ is imitated by Satan: conversion, spiritual gifts, healing, miracles, release from fear—he counterfeits them all. His offer to me of light and peace was nothing more than a shimmering mirage. And as those who live in the desert know, mistaking a mirage for reality can be fatal. It is no less true in the spiritual world. Had I not rejected the devil's offer, I shudder to think of the consequences.

Recognizing the "presence" of light as Satan, ordering him to be gone, and rejecting the mirage of peace did not, however, rid me of depression. To be healed, I had to go one step further. This involved humbly kneeling and allowing one of God's servants to be a channel for God's power through prayer and laying on of hands. That proved to be the key which unlocked the prison, allowing the supernatural inflow of God's love to cast out the terrible tormenting fear. Only then was I able to accept God's love in the breaking experiences. And only then did I find genuine freedom from depression, and the reality of God's peace within.

Those who mistake the mirage Satan conjures up—a being of light who totally and unconditionally accepts the dying, ushering them into a state of eternal bliss—for reality, say they no longer fear death. But common sense tells us, to be rid of any fear without being rid of the causing factor incurs a far greater peril.

It is not enough to recognize Satan's disguise and reject the mirage. We must meet God's conditions, not circumventing the Cross, which alone confers the certainty of life everlasting. The glorious word is that Jesus shared our humanity *"so that by his death he might destroy him who holds the power of death—that is, the devil—and free those who all their lives were held in slavery by their fear of death."*[29] Christ alone can legitimately and redemptively free us from the fear of death.

Does this mean all edge-of-death experiences are hallucinations or Satan's mirages? Not at all. In fact, the counterfeit inevitably presupposes there is the real.

Moments before his death, Stephen looked into the eternal heavens and saw Jesus standing at the right hand of God the Father. Paul, Peter, James, and John had heavenly visions. There is no reason to reject the possibility that even today dying Christians see beyond death's door into the heavenly places. And, too, that some persons who have not made their peace with God have bona-fide visions of hell. Why some do and others don't, we simply do not know.

How should you and I view these other-world experiences?

In Acts 15, when the Jerusalem council was establishing the doctrine of the Early Church, Peter and Paul told of their experiences, while James quoted Scripture to back them up. This indicates that examining personal experience can be useful in understanding biblical truths, but we must be wary. Truth is not built on the foundation of subjective experience—our own or others'. Rather, truth is the foundation on which we stand to examine all subjective experience. All subjective experience—visions, dreams, personal perceptions, intuitional concepts—whatever occurs at variance with the Scriptures, must be flatly rejected as fantasy.

We must stay alert to the possibility of Satan's intrusion, if not in some visual form of light, then, more often, as some "enlightening" thought or message. His manifestation may be fascinating, easily catching our imagination or interest. But one thing is certain. As we come to know God more and more, as His radiance increasingly fills our lives, we will be far less inclined to go chasing after Satan's counterfeits—whatever form they may take. Death will hold no terror, nor will life's challenges cause us to panic, for God himself will direct our coming in and our going out.[30]

Epilogue

Reading back over the pages of this book, I realize that identifying certain distorted teachings with the renewal movement could leave a false impression. These deceptions are not unique to a particular spiritual climate nor should we relegate them to a particular period of church history. Satan's deceptions are much like a kaleidoscope: as the tube is rotated, exactly the same bits of colored glass form each new design. Even so, Satan's deceptions have certain constants. He cashes in on our fears, our pride, and our desire for power and control. He takes advantage of our need for love, our religious orientation and our desire to know God. And he capitalizes on our attempts to impress others by some lofty revelation; he uses the tendency some have to carry a good thing to extreme. Whatever the time frame, Satan's usual methods are the "bits of colored glass" he employs to concoct his myriad of deceptions. If we keep in mind these constants, we will be quicker to recognize his counterfeits regardless of what form they take.

Spiritual health and maturity entail much more, though, than simply steering clear of Satan's enticing doctrines. Positive steps need to be taken if we are to become the people God has called us to be and to participate in establishing His kingdom. It's essential, too, that we keep informed as to what is happening to the Church at any particular moment. Even now.

I, and many others, believe that both the charismatic renewal that began in the mid-sixties, and the revival of evangelism that simultaneously occurred in many churches not identified with

209

the pentecostal experience—have in some aspects peaked. In fact, when various church authorities took it upon themselves to "legitimize" the work of the Holy Spirit in an effort to keep their sheep in the home pasture, the downward slide began. A few leaders attempted to assume command and establish an organization of the spiritually elite. At the same time, our unfortunate labeling of "Methodist Charismatics," "Catholic Charismatics," "Baptist Charismatics," "Lutheran Charismatics," and "Non-Charismatics," along with the excesses and extremes and the factions that sometimes occurred, were enough to signal an early demise of the beautiful, spontaneous movement of the Holy Spirit sweeping through the land.

The question that now faces us is: Where do we go from here?

We must begin by examining the ultimate purpose of God for His Church. That purpose will show us the steps we must take to flow with God in fulfilling His purpose.

To help us understand God's purpose for the Church in this critical hour, it's helpful to look at Israel's history—for Israel likewise had a covenant relationship with God. Tracing Israel's lifeline through the Old Testament, we find it archs to glorious highs, plummets to shameful lows, and drifts across broad plateaus of apathy—not unlike the lifeline of the Church.

Reading through the Prophets, we find Israel slogging around in a morass of moral debauchery; priests and people are embroiled in false religions, her leaders are thoroughly corrupt, and spiritual blindness and deafness are epidemic.

But what does God say?

For one thing, although the nation is ripe for judgment, there is a remnant in the land who has never bowed the knee to the gods of pleasure, lust, greed and injustice. They are Jehovah's pride and joy! Further, God says when judgment falls, there will always be an element of mercy. For always God's ultimate purpose is to *redeem, restore* and *establish His people in righteousness.* This was His purpose for Israel; this is His purpose for His Church.

God does have a company of righteous people who faithfully represent Him in a world gone morally mad. But, at the same time, there are those shackled by chains forged from deceptive teaching and the devil's trickery who need to be *redeemed*. Certainly, wherever fragmentation has occurred, the Church needs *restoration*. But above all, if the Church is to be the embodiment of all that Christ is, the members of His body must exemplify His *righteousness*; we must be *right* before God, *right* with others, *right* at the core.

Under the old covenant, Israel utterly failed to fulfill the righteous demands of the law. But under the new covenant, through the ministry of the Spirit, we find in Jesus Christ all the righteousness the law demanded. This righteousness must be carefully understood.

The marvelous thing God does for us when we place our faith in the sacrificial death of Jesus in our behalf is to *declare us righteous* and, thereby, free from guilt and punishment for our sins. This is known as *imputed* righteousness. But righteousness is also to be fulfilled in us.' This means we are to express God's righteousness by our priorities, our goals, our total life-style—by every choice we make, everything we say or do.

But does the Church, in fact, exemplify the righteous character of a holy God?

Frequently the evidence points to the contrary. Although integrity is an essential component of righteousness, it is a virtue often deplorably lacking in professing Christians. Recently the gravity of the problem was underscored when a missionary statesman announced that the organization he represents would no longer do business with Christian vendors or professional people. He explained:

> They promise things they have neither the competence nor training nor intent to deliver. We have found the unbelievers . . . much more responsible, reliable, competent and willing to do what they contract to do.
> It should be remembered that promises, contracts, and oaths are the acts of will and intelligence that make a society coherent, that holds it together. If they cannot be trusted then the whole structure begins to fall.[2]

Of all people, a Christian should be a person of unquestioned integrity, absolutely honest and genuine. Integrity means not taking advantage of someone in order to make a good business deal; it means not using people. It means not appropriating supplies from one's employer to make up for low wages. Integrity means keeping appointments on time, paying one's bills, paying one's taxes. It means making restitution. It means keeping one's word whether or not it is convenient. *Integrity means fulfilling righteousness.*

Think of what might happen if every single person praying the Lord's Prayer truly meant, "Thy kingdom come. Thy will be done in earth. . . ." The prospect is mind-boggling!

As it is, some just parrot the words. Others think in terms of some vague future event. But the spiritually perceptive person knows there is both the future and present aspect of the kingdom. He knows that to sincerely pray, "Thy kingdom come . . ." is to abdicate self-rule, enthrone Jesus Christ, and bring every aspect of life under His rule. "A king will rule in righteousness," proclaimed the prophet Isaiah. "He will reign . . ." over his kingdom, establishing and upholding it with justice and righteousness.[3] To live under Christ's rule is to live righteously—not necessarily sensationally.

Joel's prophecy (chapter 2) is a favorite quote to prove that before Christ's return we shall see spectacular phenomena as a demonstration of God's power and glory. But many more Scriptures indicate a mighty revival of righteousness as God's end design for His Church. When "the Spirit is poured upon us from on high," declared Isaiah, "justice will dwell in the desert and *righteousness* will be peace; the effect of *righteousness* will be quietness and confidence forever."[4] (Emphasis mine.)

The basic principle expounded by Isaiah is that "peace is not a thing God superimposes on a corrupt society; the ground must be cleared and resown with righteousness, of which peace is the fruit."[5]

A visitation of God does sometimes include the spectacular. But only a world-sweeping revival of righteousness will change the Church from a shoddy caricature of the Bride of Christ into a Church pure and spotless, ready to receive Christ the Bridegroom when He comes to claim His Beloved.

Now back to the question: What steps must we take to flow

with God in fulfilling His purpose for the Church? Let me suggest five important actions:

1. *Guard against deception*; important ways are described throughout this book.

2. *Handle the Word with scrupulous honesty.* Heed Paul's counsel: "Do your best to present yourself to God as one approved, a workman who does not need to be ashamed and who correctly handles the word of truth."[6]

3. *Live righteously*, fulfilling the righteousness of Christ imputed to us. Be a person of unquestionable integrity.

4. *Beware of a critical spirit.* Don't become so obsessed with denouncing deception and hypocrisy that you fall into this trap.

5. *Remember Who is our hope.* Though God longs to perfect His Church, our hope is not in the consummation of a perfect Church. Our hope is in the Perfect One. And loving obedience to Christ is to be our all-consuming passion.

So where do we go from here?

As redeemed men and women being transformed into the image of Jesus and living righteously, we can walk confidently into the future, knowing and rejoicing that *"The path of the righteous is like the first gleam of dawn, shining ever brighter till the full light of day."*[7]

Notes

Introduction

1. *Exorcism,* ed. Dom Robert Petitpierre, O.S.B. (SPCK). Quoted by John Richards, *Deliver Us From Evil.* New York: The Seabury Press, 1974, p. 19. Copyright 1974 by John Richards.
2. Ibid., p. 134.
3. Malachi 4:5 notes Elijah's expected appearance before the coming of the Messiah. Revelation 11 speaks of "two witnesses." One of these witnesses is generally accepted to be Elijah. The prophecy of end-times events depicts two witnesses killed and their bodies left lying in the street. Men would gaze upon them and refuse them burial. But after three and a half days, God would breathe life into them. And they would be caught up to heaven while their enemies looked on.
4. 2 Tim. 4:3-5.
5. 2 Tim. 1:8.
6. 2 Tim. 4:5.
7. E. Stanley Jones, *A Song of Ascents.* Nashville: Abingdon, 1968, p. 224. Used by permission of Abingdon Press.
8. Ibid.
9. Rev. 4:8.
10. Matt. 7:14 (NASB).

Chapter One

1. 2 Cor. 9:6.
2. Luke 9:62.
3. Mal. 3:10 (KJV).
4. Acts 3:6.
5. James 5:1-3, 5.

214

6. 1 Cor. 4:11.
7. 1 Cor. 4:16, 17.
8. 2 Cor. 9:11.
9. Cynthia R. Schaible, "The Gospel of the Good Life," *Eternity,* February 1981, p. 22. Reprinted by permission of *Eternity* magazine, Copyright 1981, Evangelical Ministries, Inc., 1716 Spruce Street, Philadelphia, PA 19103.
10. 1 Tim. 6:5.
11. Gal. 6:10.
12. Matt. 6:24; Luke 16:13.
13. 1 Tim. 6:9.
14. 1 Tim. 6:10.
15. Prov. 30:5.
16. Prov. 30:7-9.
17. Matt. 6:11.
18. 2 Cor. 9:11.
19. Luke 6:38.
20. Isa. 54:2.
21. 2 Cor. 6:10 (KJV).
22. Luke 6:35, 36.
23. Gen. 17:1.
24. Matt. 6:33.
25. Matt. 6:32.
26. 2 Cor. 12:7-9.
27. Ps. 37:4.
28. Ps. 37:16, 17.
29. 1 Tim. 6:6.
30. A. W. Tozer, *I Talk Back to the Devil.* Harrisburg: Christian Publications, Inc., 1972, pp. 30, 31. Used by permission.

Chapter Two

1. 1 Cor. 4:6.
2. 1 Thess. 5:18.
3. Eph. 5:20 (KJV).
4. Isa. 5:20.
5. 2 Cor. 2:4.
6. Mark 15:34.
7. Ronald M. Enroth and Gerald E. Jamison, *The Gay Church.*

Grand Rapids: Eerdmans, 1974, p. 52. Used by permission of Wm. B. Eerdmans Publishing Co.

8. James 1:8.
9. 1 John 3:8.
10. 2 Cor. 5:17.
11. Ps. 107:10, 11, 13-16.
12. Eph. 5:20.
13. 1 John 2:16.
14. James 1:13-15.
15. Matt. 7:21-23.
16. Ps. 78:34, 36, 37.
17. Ps. 4:5.
18. Lev. 22:29.
19. Ps. 97:10.
20. Ps. 126:6 (KJV).
21. Ps. 63:2-4, 7.
22. Ps. 59:1, 16, 17.
23. Ps. 33:1.
24. Ps. 119:7.

Chapter Three

1. Michael Rothenberg, *Psychology Encyclopedia.* Guilford, Connecticut: The Dushkin Publishing Group, Inc., 1973, p. 123.
2. 1 Cor. 1:12 (RSV; *follow*, NIV).
3. 1 Cor. 3:18-21 (RSV).
4. Rom. 12:3.
5. Num. 21:8.
6. 2 Kings 18:4.
7. 1 Kings 12:28-30.
8. Ex. 16:27.
9. 2 Pet. 1:1.
10. 2 Pet. 1:5-7.

Chapter Four

1. *Encyclopedic Dictionary of Religion.* Washington, D.C.: Corpus Publications, 1980, s.v. "ecstasies," A. P. Hanlon. Used by permission.

2. Rev. 1:17.
3. 2 Chron. 5:14 (KJV).
4. William James, *The Varieties of Religious Experience.* New York, The New American Library, Inc., 1958, pp. 313, 314.
5. *Encyclopaedia of Religion and Ethics.* New York: Charles Scribner's Sons, 1914, p. 158, s.v. "ecstasies."
6. Ibid.
7. W. A. McKay, *Outpourings of the Spirit.* Philadelphia: Presbyterian Board of Publication and Sabbath-School Work, 1890, pp. 59, 68.
8. Ex. 7, 8.
9. *Encyclopaedia of Religion and Ethics,* s.v. "ecstasies."
10. J. Aumann, *Encyclopedic Dictionary of Religion,* p. 1155.
11. McKay, *Outpourings of the Spirit,* p. 67.
12. Agatha Christie, *Agatha Christie: An Autobiography.* New York: Dodd, Mead. Copyright Agatha Christie, 1977, p. 72. Used by permission of the Christie estate.
13. John 14:27.
14. Rom. 5:1.
15. Phil. 4:7.
16. G. G. Findley, "Fruit of the Spirit," *Exposition of the Bible.* Hartford, Conn.: Scranton, 1903.
17. Ninian Smart, *The Religious Experience of Mankind.* New York: Charles Scribner's Sons, 1969, p. 474. 1 John 4:18.
18. John 16:33.
19. 2 Cor. 6:4.
20. 2 Cor. 2:14.

Chapter Five
1. Acts 20:30.
2. 1 Tim. 5:14 (RSV).
3. 1 Tim. 3:4, 5.
4. 1 Pet. 3:5.
5. 1 Pet. 3:6.
6. Gen. 15:2-5 (author's paraphrase).
7. Gen. 16:2.
8. Gen. 17:15, 16 (author's paraphrase).
9. Gen. 21:10.

218

10. Gen. 21:12.
11. Ibid.
12. Gen. 24:18.
13. Gen. 12:17-19; 20:2-7.
14. Prov. 12:22.
15. Rev. 22:15.
16. Acts 5.
17. 1 Tim. 2:5.
18. James Lee Beall, *Your Pastor, Your Shepherd.* Plainfield, N.J.: Logos, 1977, p. 203. Quoted by permission.
19. 2 Tim. 2:1.
20. 2 Tim. 2:15.
21. 1 Tim. 2:5.
22. 2 Tim. 1:14.
23. Matt. 18:5.
24. Eph. 5:21; 1 Pet. 5:5; 1 Cor. 16:16; as it relates to Rom. 16:3.
25. Matt. 18:19.
26. 1 Pet. 3:7.
27. 1 Cor. 11:3-5, 7.
28. Lee Anna Starr, *The Bible Status of Women.* Old Tappan, N.J.: Revell, 1926; Zarephath, N.J.: Pillar of Fire, 1955, pp. 296-299. Used by permission.
29. 1 Cor. 11:10.
30. Starr, *Bible Status of Women,* pp. 305, 310.
31. Ps. 91:1, 4, 9, 10.
32. John 17:15.
33. 2 Thess. 3:3.
34. Phil. 4:7.
35. Beall, *Your Pastor, Your Shepherd,* pp. 203, 204.
36. Gal. 3:26-28.
37. 1 Thess. 5:21.

Chapter Six

1. Eccles. 5:5.
2. Gene Church & Conrad D. Carnes, *The Pit.* New York, Outerbridge & Lazard, Inc., 1972: N.Y. Dutton Pocket Books. Quoted by permission of Gene Church, Author's Preface.
3. Ibid., p. vii.

4. Church & Carnes, *The Pit,* p. vii.
5. Prov. 27:21.
6. Rom. 16:18.
7. Jude 16.
8. John 8:32.
9. Matt. 20:25, 26.
10. Ps. 40:8 (KJV).
11. Ps. 25:9.

Chapter Seven

1. 1 Cor. 10:13 (RSV).
2. 1 Cor. 10:14 (*Therefore, my beloved,* RSV; *flee from idolatry,* NIV).
3. Prov. 25:17 (NASB).
4. Phil. 2:13 (author's paraphrase).
5. Rom. 5:5.

Chapter Eight

1. Matt. 18:16.
2. 1 Sam. 15:23 (KJV).
3. Matt. 12:44, 45.
4. 1 Sam. 9:21.
5. 1 Sam. 15:10-15 (author's paraphrase).
6. 1 Sam. 15:22.
7. 1 Sam. 15:23.
8. 1 Sam. 31:6.
9. A. J. Russell, ed., *God Calling,* by Two Listeners. Old Tappan, N.J.: Fleming H. Revell—A Spire book; first published by Dodd, Mead & Co., 1936. Used by permission.
10. Ibid., Preface.
11. Ibid., Introduction by Russell.
12. Ibid.
13. Ibid., p. 70.
14. Ibid., p. 19.
15. Ibid., p. 171.
16. Heb. 12:2.
17. *God Calling,* p. 145.
18. Deut. 18:10; Ex. 22:18; Lev. 20:27.

19. Isa. 8:19.
20. Isa. 8:20, 22.
21. *God Calling,* p. 52.
22. A. J. Russell, ed., *God at Eventide,* by Two Listeners. New York: Dodd, Mead & Co., 1950, p. 92. Used by permission.
23. Rom. 12:15 (author's paraphrase).
24. *God Calling,* p. 202.
25. 1 Tim. 6:12.
26. 1 John 4:18.
27. *God Calling,* p. 17.
28. 1 John 4:1.
29. *God Calling,* Preface.
30. Ps. 19:7-11.
31. Matt. 28:20.
32. John 8:19 (author's paraphrase).
33. John 10:14.
34. Heb. 5:14.

Chapter Nine

 1. 2 Cor. 6:14.
 2. 2 Cor. 6:14-16.
 3. Luke 6:30 (KJV).
 4. Ezek. 22:28, 31.
 5. 2 Pet. 2:3.
 6. 2 Pet. 2:3 (NEB).
 7. 1 Cor. 14:3.
 8. Deut. 18:22.
 9. 1 Cor. 7:15.
10. Jer. 23:14, 16.
11. Jer. 23:31.
12. Jer. 8:11.
13. Jer. 23:17.
14. Jer. 13:11, 14.
15. Jer. 14:15, 16.
16. Eph. 5:3, 6.
17. 1 John 1:9.
18. Isa. 29:15, 20.
19. Josh. 1:5.

20. Josh. 7:12.
21. Josh. 7:10-15 (author's paraphrase).
22. Deut. 7:7, 9.
23. 2 Pet. 2:20, 21.
24. 2 Tim. 2:12, 13.
25. Jer. 9:24.
26. D. Guthrie & J. A. Moyer, eds., *The New Bible Commentary: Revised.* Grand Rapids: Wm. B. Eerdmans Publishing Co., p. 1179. The Pastoral Epistles by A. M. Stibbs.
27. Ps. 136.
28. Florence Bulle, *Lord of the Valleys.* Plainfield, N.J.: Logos, 1972: Bridge, 1982, p. 71.
29. 1 John 4:18 (*casts out,* RSV; *drives out,* NIV; *all,* TEV).
30. 1 Thess. 5:11.
31. Luke 17:1.
32. Jude 20, 21.

Chapter Ten

1. 1 Cor. 1:9, 20, 25.
2. Obad. 3, 4, 18.
3. Ralph Mahoney, "Taking the Spoils from Satan," *World Map Digest,* July/August 1979, p. 26. Used by permission.

Chapter Eleven

1. L. Nelson Bell, *While Men Slept.* Garden City, N.Y.: Doubleday & Co., 1970, p. 19. Reprinted from *Christianity Today.*
2. Ps. 51:10 (KJV).
3. Gal. 3:3.
4. Num. 14:8, 9.
5. Ps. 68:6 (KJV).
6. Ps. 107:35.
7. "Because He Lives," by William J. and Gloria Gaither, Copyright 1971. Reprinted by permission of The Benson Company, Inc.
8. E. Stanley Jones, *A Song of Ascents.* Nashville: Abingdon, 1968, p. 224.
9. Ibid., p. 225.

10. Rev. 12:9, 10; John 14:26 (KJV).
11. 2 Tim. 4:2.
12. Rom. 12:1, 2.
13. Edward Shorter, *The Making of the Modern Family.* New York: Basic Books, 1975, p. 278. Used by permission.
14. John 5:19 (author's paraphrase).
15. Bell, *While Men Slept,* p. 19.
16. Zech. 4:6.

Chapter Twelve

1. 2 Cor. 11:15, 13.
2. Raymond A. Moody, Jr., *Life After Life.* New York: Bantam, 1976, pp. 22, 23.
3. Maurice Rawlings, *Beyond Death's Door.* Nashville: Thomas Nelson, 1978. Dr. Maurice S. Rawlings is a specialist in cardiovascular diseases at the Diagnostic Hospital in Chattanooga, Tennessee. He is a member of numerous medical organizations, including the American Heart Association, the American College of Physicians, the American College of Chest Physicians, the American College of Cardiology, and the American Society of Internal Medicine.
4. Ibid., p. 21.
5. Ibid., pp. 21, 22.
6. Ibid., pp. 64, 66.
7. Rom. 3:4.
8. Heb. 9:27.
9. 2 Thess. 1:8, 9.
10. John 8:12.
11. John 8:21, 22, 24.
12. Moody, *Life After Life,* pp. 58, 59. 61.
13. Acts 17:31.
14. Matt. 25:41, 46.
15. Stephen C. Board, "Light at the End of the Tunnel," *Eternity,* July 1977, p. 15. Reprinted by permission of *Eternity* magazine, Copyright 1981, Evangelical Ministries, Inc., 1716 Spruce Street, Philadelphia, Pa. 19103.
16. Gal. 1:6-8.
17. Elizabeth Kübler-Ross, *On Death and Dying.* New York: Macmillan, 1969, chaps. 3-7.

23

223

18. Ann Nietzke, "The Miracle of Kübler-Ross," *Human Behavior,* September 1977, p. 25. Used by permission of Manson Western Corporation, 12031 Wilshire Blvd., Los Angeles, Calif. 90025.
19. Ibid., p. 23.
20. John 8:12.
21. Nietzke, p. 24.
22. Ibid., p. 24.
23. Ibid., pp. 25, 27.
24. Books reviewed by Dale Sanders, *Christianity Today,* 17 June 1977, p. 33.
25. "The Conversion of Kübler-Ross," *Time,* 12 November 1979, p. 81.
26. Robert M. Herhold, "Kübler-Ross and Life After Death," *The Christian Century.* 14 April 1976, p. 363. Copyright 1976, Christian Century Foundation. Reprinted by permission from the April 14, 1976 issue of *The Christian Century.*
27. Ibid., p. 364.
28. Ibid.
29. Heb. 2:14, 15.
30. John 10:9.

Epilogue
1. Rom. 8:4
2. Ralph Mahoney, Editorial, *World Map Digest* (Nov.-Dec., 1981). Used by permission.
3. Isa. 32:1
4. Isa. 32:15-17
5. NBCR, Derek Kider on Isaiah, p. 608
6. 2 Tim. 2:15
7. Prov. 4:18